THE OCTOPUS SCIENTISTS

Exploring the Mind of a Mollusk

Written by **Sy Montgomery**

Photographs by **Keith Ellenbogen**

Houghton Mifflin Harcourt
Boston New York

To Wilson Menashi, who taught me so much about octopuses. —S.M.
To a future diver and underwater explorer, my loving niece, Maya Ellenbogen. —K.E.

Text copyright © 2015 by Sy Montgomery
Photographs copyright © 2015 by Keith Ellenbogen

For information about permission to reproduce selections from this book, write to trade.permissions@hmhco.com or to Permissions, Houghton Mifflin Harcourt Publishing Company, 3 Park Avenue, 19th Floor, New York, New York 10016.

www.hmhco.com

The text of this book is set in Scala.
Map illustration by Rachel Newborn
Octopus tattoo diagram by Dave Mahan
Sidebar border and line space illustrations by Sy Montgomery

Library of Congress Cataloging-in-Publication Data is on file.
ISBN: 978-0-544-98690-9

Manufactured in USA
PHX 10 9 8 7 6 5 4 3 2 1
4500613976

CONTENTS

An octopus hiding in his home. Can you find him?

- 1   CHAPTER 1
- 7   *Meet the Octopus Team*
- 11   *An Octet of Octo Facts*
- 13   CHAPTER 2
- 18   *CRIOBE*
- 21   CHAPTER 3
- 25   *How Smart Is an Octopus?*
- 27   CHAPTER 4
- 32   *Making Friends with an Octopus*
- 35   CHAPTER 5
- 42   *How Octopuses Change Color*
- 45   CHAPTER 6
- 50   *Rainforests of the Oceans*
- 53   CHAPTER 7
- 58   *Octopus Influence*
- 61   CHAPTER 8
- 68   *Selected Bibliography*
- 69   *Acknowledgments*
- 70   *Index*

CHAPTER 1

The ocean is the world's largest wilderness, covering 70 percent of the surface of the globe. But this vast blue territory is even bigger than it looks from land, or even from space. It's a three-dimensional realm that accounts for more than 95 percent of all livable space on the planet—and most of it is unexplored.

The sea is home to creatures whose weirdness rivals that of the strangest sci-fi aliens anyone ever imagined. We're searching for one of them now: an animal with a baggy, boneless body, eight sucker-laden arms attached to its head, a beak like a parrot, and venom like a snake. It can shift its shape, change its color, squirt ink, and pour itself through the tiniest opening—or shoot away through the sea by squirting water out of a flexible funnel, or jet, on the side of its head.

We're looking for octopuses—the Pacific day octopus, to be exact, one of perhaps 250 octopus species on the planet. Pacific day octopuses grow to more than four feet long. They're not rare or endangered. Should be pretty easy to find, right?

"Ptttttthhhth!"

A spout like a small whale's shoots from her snorkel as Jennifer Mather pulls her silver-haired head from the water. She looks through her prescription facemask and waits for the rest of us to surface from the sea. Soon we answer her with a chorus of spouts.

Jennifer pulls the snorkel from her mouth. "Find anything?" she asks.

Around us stretches a tropical paradise of palm-fringed mountains. The island's waters teem with fish in neon colors and fantastic shapes. Honeymooners seek its warm blue sea, white beaches, and Polynesian food. But that's not what drew our team of six from three countries to the shallows here surrounding Moorea, a fifty-square-mile, roughly heart-shaped island twelve miles northwest of its much larger

Jennifer Mather.

An octopus can jet away faster than a human swimmer can follow.

neighbor, Tahiti, in the South Pacific.

No—we are out here looking for holes. Because where there's a hole, there might be an octopus.

"That hole in the middle of that dead coral looks good," says Jennifer, pointing. Near it, she has found an empty shell. She holds it up to show us. That makes *two* pieces of evidence that suggest we could be closing in on our quarry. But it won't be as easy as it might seem.

What does our octopus look like? Well, that's the problem: *Octopus cyanea* (it's named after Cyane, a water nymph in Greek mythology) might be fat and red, skinny and white, tall and brown, or a combination of colors and shapes. It might have stripes or spots or splotches—and then, the next second, it might look completely different. Or become utterly invisible.

Not only can it squeeze its three-foot-long arms and melon-size body through a hole the size of a thimble; it can also hide in plain sight. As well as changing color to match its surroundings, it can instantly sprout little projections all over its skin called papillae (pa-PIL-ay) to make it look exactly like a piece of algae or coral or rock.

Which is what the octopuses in this part of Opunohu Bay may be doing at this very moment—if they're here at all.

"Octopuses are hard to find," concedes Jennifer. Though she works at the University of Lethbridge in the center of Canada, far from any ocean, she's been probing the mysteries of these quirky, changeable animals for forty years. She's conducted experiments with the giant Pacific octopus, which can grow to more than one hundred pounds, in the Seattle Aquarium. She's studied the five-inch-long pygmy octopus in Florida and the common octopus in Bermuda. And she's watched the Pacific day octopus before, off the island of Hawaii, and the common octopus off the Caribbean island of Bonaire.

Everything about them fascinates her, but especially this: "Octopuses are smart," she says—and that's thought to be rare for invertebrates (in-VERT-a-brits). Invertebrates include insects, spiders, worms, snails, starfish, and clams; they have no bones, and usually have a very small brain. (Starfish and clams have no brain at all!)

Octopuses are in fact related to snails and clams—they're all mollusks. Most mollusks have shells—but not octos. That makes the octopus an unprotected packet of tasty protein for predators. Almost anything big enough can eat an octopus: along with its cousin, squid, it is the main prey of marine mammals, sharks, and many fish. Humans eat them too.

But what the octopus lacks in protective shell it makes up for in smarts. Actually, having no shell might be the very reason octopuses are so smart: they have to be. If you're a clam, you can just sit around, wait for food to float to you, and depend on your shell to protect you. Leaving the ancestral shell behind allowed octopuses more active lives, but also brought dangers demanding snap judgments. If a hungry shark approaches, should the octopus hide in a hole? Change color or shape? Release a smokescreen of ink? Or squirt a hanging blob of ink that looks like an octopus—while the octopus itself jets away?

To both hunt and hide, an octopus must choose wisely among many options, and it has evolved a big brain to help it do so. Jenni-

A small decorator crab might make a nice snack for an octopus.

fer, a professor of psychology, is interested in how these intelligent invertebrates make decisions. That's why she's invited a team of octopus experts here to Moorea: to find out how octopuses decide what to eat . . . while avoiding being eaten themselves.

What good can come from studying the life of an octopus? "There is an appalling amount we don't know about the ocean," says Jennifer—so much so that the most elementary research might lead to unexpected breakthroughs.

Jennifer points out that people are already using knowledge of octopuses to model "soft" robots, which roam over rough ground much better than vehicles with wheels. And that's only a beginning. "Octopuses' arms are full of suction cups that are marvels of manipulation," she notes. "How come we're not copying them? Well, because we don't understand them." Another marvel: Female octopuses deactivate and store sperm from the males for months—then activate the sperm when the moment is right to lay eggs. Talk about family planning! Jennifer wonders, "How come we aren't finding out how they do that?"

But perhaps even more important than helping us design new gadgets or even improve our medical knowledge, studying octopuses may provide answers to some of life's most intriguing questions. Octopuses represent a different route to high intelligence—which is why Jennifer was asked to give a talk about them for the SETI (Search for Extra Terrestrial Intelligence) Institute. Might extraterrestrials look and act more like octopuses than like us?

"What are the possibilities of life on earth?" asks Jennifer. "Lots—and we'll only know by finding out about marine animals."

Dripping with seawater, she holds up for our inspection the two-inch shell she has found. "Is this a drill hole?" she asks. "I can't tell."

David Scheel leans his six-foot frame down to look. A behavioral ecologist and an expert on the giant Pacific octopus, David is a professor of marine biology at Alaska Pacific University in Anchorage. He's seen lots of drill holes. Drilling is one of several ways the ingenious octopus can get at the tasty meat inside even the strongest shells.

Sometimes an octopus can just pop the two halves of a clam's shell open with its strong suckers. With just one of its biggest suckers, one of David's giants can lift up to thirty pounds. Or the octopus might chip at a shell with its beak, which is as strong as a parrot's. If the shell is too thick, the octo might drill. On its tongue an octopus has a ribbon of teeth called a radula (RAD-jula), an organ unique to mollusks, which the octopus uses to drill holes and other mollusks use to shred prey. And the octo has another trick up its sleeve: it can dissolve the calcium in the shell by squirting it with acid from a gland in the front of its head. Once the hole is deep enough, the octopus can inject venom from a different gland, one in the back of its head, through the hole to paralyze the prey. The venom even starts dissolving the meal, the way meat-tenderizing enzymes work on a juicy steak.

But whoever ate the mollusk who lived in this shell apparently didn't drill. "No," says David, after a careful look, "I don't see a hole. But look what I found!" Just minutes ago he was investigating another possible octopus home—a crevice under a rock—and he collected what he found just outside it. He unfolds his palm and reveals the orange claw and shell (also called a carapace) of a crab. The claw was piled on top of the carapace, and both of them on top of a clam shell. Nobody in the sea is tidier than an octopus!

Lots of different items may appear on an octopus's menu—everything from clams to snails to fellow octopuses. (This is a hazard for an octopus seeking a mate; their first date could be dinner, with one of them being the main course!) Giant Pacific octopuses sometimes catch and eat birds. One was seen dining on an otter (who was probably dead when the octopus found it).

But crabs are among octopuses' very favorite foods. And the remains of this crab bear the signature of an octopus—as Tatiana Leite, a marine ecologist from Brazil, confirms the moment David hands his find to her. Beneath her facemask, the edges of Tatiana's brown eyes crinkle as she smiles. "Yeah!" she agrees. "It's intact, and the inside is completely clean. A fish would have crunched it all up."

Jennifer, David, and Tatiana share the same mission: to find out what the Pacific day octopuses of Moorea are eating, and why. But each scientist views this mysterious study animal through a slightly different lens. Jennifer, the head of our team, as a psychologist, is convinced that each octopus's personality plays an important role in food choices. She expects that bolder, more adventurous octopuses will venture farther from their dens and choose a wider variety of prey. David's specialty is behavioral ecology. He's fascinated by the dynamics of predators and their prey. He suspects that octopuses prefer big crabs but those who can't find and catch them make do with smaller prey and a wider menu. As a marine ecologist, Tatiana is especially interested in how an animal's environment affects how it behaves. She predicts that the octopuses who live in a more complex and varied environment will have a more diverse diet.

Which of these theories is correct may be important for many different reasons. But one reason is that finding out what octopuses eat and why might help scientists discover whether octopus populations are in danger or not. Octopuses, as we can see, are very difficult to count. That makes it hard to tell whether any octopus species are endangered or declining. Some species in some areas might be: the common octopus might be overfished in some waters; other kinds, such as the exceptionally beautiful mimic octopus, could be overcollected for the saltwater aquarium trade. Other threats, such as pollution and global warming, might be hurting octopus species too—either by harming them directly or by affecting their favorite prey. Is there enough food for each octopus species? Nobody knows—or can even begin to find out—until scientists discover exactly what they all eat and why. This study might well turn out to be a model for other studies on different octopus species elsewhere.

At Jennifer's invitation, each researcher has come here to test his or her own idea, or hypothesis. A new scuba diver from New Hampshire who has never snorkeled before, I've joined the team to write this book about their quest; Keith Ellenbogen, an underwater photographer and expert scuba diver and snorkeler, came along from New York to take the pictures on these pages. Soon another researcher, Keely Langford, an eagle-eyed interpreter with the Vancouver Aquarium in Canada, will join us to help.

There's lots to do. We'll be collecting and classifying the shells around octopuses' homes. We'll be carefully surveying the plants, animals, and rocks on the sea bottom where the octopuses live. We even plan to give each octopus we find a personality test!

But first we have to find the shape-shifting, hole-hiding octopuses—animals who are masters of escape and disguise.

"I think an octopus had a meal here, without a doubt," says David.

The question is: Where is it now?

MEET THE OCTOPUS TEAM

Name: Jennifer Mather
Age: 69
Nationality: Canadian
Job: Professor of Psychology, University of Lethbridge, Alberta, Canada

Growing up on the west coast of Canada, Jennifer was always outdoors—and often on or in the water. She was the third of three sisters (a brother came along nine years after Jennifer was born) but liked being alone in nature. She built a fort in the woods, watched and identified birds, and learned the names of all the wildflowers. She loved the seashore best, collecting shells, turning over rocks to see who was hiding beneath, dropping small pebbles onto sea anemones to see what the creatures would do. By age ten she knew she wanted to study the sea's animals for the rest of her life.

But back in the 1960s, when Jennifer went to college, marine biology—in fact, field studies of all kinds—was considered a young man's field, one that women shouldn't enter. Jennifer was turned down for a graduate program in conservation and thrown out of one professor's marine laboratory in graduate school. Back then, women were more welcome in the "helping professions," such as nursing and teaching. Jennifer's Ph.D. research focused on human sensory-motor coordination, which later led her to study the eye movements of people with the mental illness schizophrenia. Meanwhile, she set up a tank for pygmy octopuses in the basement of the psychology building at Brandeis University to observe what they were doing.

Since then, Jennifer has built on her earlier work in psychology to become a specialist in how humans perceive the world, how people coordinate senses with movement, and how humans' minds change and grow throughout life. At the same time, she's continued and expanded her studies of octopuses in the wild and in aquariums. Her particular area of interest? How octopuses use their minds to think, solve problems, and develop individual personalities.

It's a revolutionary idea. Twenty years ago, most researchers wouldn't even admit that octopuses have personalities—much less try to study them. But to Jennifer, as well as to many others who keep octopuses, that each octopus has a distinct and unique personality is obvious. One giant Pacific octopus Jennifer met was so shy that she hid behind the filter pump all the time; Seattle Aquarium staff named her Emily Dickinson, after the reclusive poet. (Eventually they let the octopus go in Puget Sound.) Another was so bold, he came up to greet his handlers when they opened the top of his tank, wrapping his arms all over his visitors and embracing them with his suckers. Aquarium keepers named him Leisure Suit Larry because he couldn't keep his "hands" to himself.

With her Seattle colleague Roland Anderson, Jennifer documented how octopuses easily recognize individual humans (even when they're identically dressed) and favor those they like; she has written papers about octopuses playing with toys; and she has created a personality test for octopuses, ranking each from bold to shy. "There's nobody doing what I'm doing," she says. "It may be weird—but it's unique!"

These days, as the first woman professor in the University of Lethbridge's Psychology Department (and the only woman in the department for the first eight of her twenty-seven years there), she's also become an advocate for women in science—as well as an advocate for humane treatment in the laboratory for invertebrates such as octopuses.

Name: David Scheel
Age: 51
Nationality: American
Job: Professor of Marine Biology and Director of the Marine Biology Program, Alaska Pacific University, Anchorage, Alaska

When David was seven years old and living with his parents and three brothers in upstate New York, he went to a movie theater for the first time. The show? *Doctor Dolittle*. "I wanted to see it," he explains, "because I already wanted to talk to the animals."

He still does.

When he was ten, David wanted to become a "mad scientist"—maybe even study space aliens. Instead, he decided to study the astonishing animals on our own planet. He moved to Tanzania in Africa to research his Ph.D. While studying lions in the Serengeti, he lived in a house with no electricity and drove a Land Rover that constantly broke down.

How do you get from African lions to Alaskan octopuses? When he returned to the States, there was no job for a lion researcher. But after the Exxon oil ship *Valdez* crashed off Alaska's shores in 1989, fouling the pristine waters of Prince William Sound, researchers were desperately needed to document its effects on the marine life there. David studied orca whales, seabirds foraging at salmon hatcheries, and octopuses—and ended up an expert on the largest octopus species on earth.

Where he works at Prince William Sound and Lower Cook Inlet, the giant Pacific octopus may grow as big as 150 pounds. The waters here are full of giants. Algae called kelp grows as tall as trees. A lion's mane jellyfish's tentacles may stretch as long as three school buses. Alaskan king crabs' legs can span five feet. Even the tides are huge: they rise and fall twenty-three feet.

In the murky, 50-degree-Farenheit water, David and his students scuba-dive to catch, release, and follow the giant octopuses to discover where they go and what they eat. David even found a way to track his octos with telemetry. (It's impossible to put a radio collar on an octopus. They don't even have a neck!) With a small needle, he pierces a hole in the octopus's gill slit and attaches a tag with a locking bolt, like a pierced earring. The tag emits a sonic ping, which he and his students can track with an underwater receiver called a directional hydrophone. This way they can find octopuses days, weeks, or months after they're tagged.

He's made some exciting discoveries in his nineteen years of work. He learned that the animals in his study may travel nearly three miles after release. He discovered that they don't crawl along the bottom as you might expect, but climb the walls of rocky shelves and ridges. He found that his study animals loved big crabs best but ate fifty-three species of prey—a seafood diet more varied than that of prehistoric humans, who, studies have found, ate just fifty kinds of marine prey over the course of thousands of years.

Surprises abound when you're studying octopuses. Once, David was tracking Jude, one of his smaller tagged study animals. Finally Jude was in sight—but he looked much bigger than before. And David couldn't see Jude's sonic tag. That's because the large octopus wasn't Jude—it was a much bigger octopus, in the process of eating him! David captured the monster, retrieved the tag from Jude's remains, and attached it to the new octopus when he released her back to the wild. One of his students named her Godzilla! (the exclamation point was part of the name). David even acknowledged her in a scientific paper he wrote in 2012: "We thank Capt. Neal Oppen for long-term contributions . . . forty octopuses for carrying our tags, and especially Jude for his sacrifice and Godzilla! for volunteering."

Tatiana Leite measures out a transect.

Name: Tatiana Leite
Age: 37
Nationality: Brazilian
Job: Professor of Marine Ecology, Federal University of Rio Grande do Norte, Natal, Brazil

When Tatiana was growing up on the tropical beach in Brazil, she loved the ocean. Her mother was always calling her to get out of the water. "And she's still trying sometimes!" Tatiana admits, laughing.

But nothing keeps Tatiana out of the water for long. When she's not scuba diving, she's snorkeling; when she's not snorkeling, she's surfing. And when she's not actually in the sea, she's teaching her students about it, or else is on her way to some new research location to study octopuses in the wild or in a lab, or to examine specimens in a museum. "The sea," she says, "is my work, my play, my passion."

As a child she first considered being a veterinarian—but hated to see animals sick and in pain. Then she was introduced to Jacques Cousteau's TV programs and discovered a happy alternative. Watching scuba divers exploring the wonders of the ocean "made it really clear" to her what she wanted to do with the rest of her life: "stay in the sea, surrounded by animals."

But she didn't meet her first octopus until college. As part of a marine biology class, her boyfriend caught one in a tide pool. "It changed color, and I was in love," she remembers. Tatiana brought it back to the house and put it in an aquarium, which she left on the kitchen counter covered with a towel. When her mother pulled the towel off and looked inside, she screamed: "An octopus in the kitchen! Aaaah!"

Every student in her college program had to choose a different species of animal to study. "Everyone else picked an easy one," she remembers—such as clams or urchins, who stay put and are easy to find. But Tatiana chose the common octopus (*Octopus vulgaris*—"vulgar" doesn't mean the octopus uses bad language; it only means it's common) that lives among the tropical reefs off Brazil's St. Peter and St. Paul Islands. The same species is found in sandy-bottomed waters off rocky coasts almost everywhere in the world except the coldest waters.

It may be common, but the common octopus is not well studied. The creature was so intriguing to Tatiana that after graduating, even though she had a job at a lab studying ocean chemistry, she "chose fun instead of money" and decided to continue studying the octopus. After analyzing twenty of the animals, Tatiana didn't think the species she was studying was the common octopus after all. Hers was stronger and more muscular than the taller, skinnier *vulgaris*. This one's beak was longer, with a sharper angle.

So, while still a master's student, Tatiana had discovered an entirely new species of octopus. Now she is working on describing five more new species of octopus off the shores of Brazil. "There is so much still to discover in the sea!" she says.

Name: Keely Langford
Age: 29
Nationality: Canadian
Job: Interpretive Specialist, Vancouver Aquarium

Keely grew up in Edmonton, Alberta, in Canada. Her best friends were the family across the street—the mom taught science and the dad was a scientist, and both kids loved science and exploration. But Keely also loved language (she went to a Mandarin immersion elementary school) and acting (she attended a performing arts high school).

Keely's dad's telecommunications job forced her family to move to Toronto when she was a junior in high school. She began college at York University there, and to earn money started working for a company called Mad Science, teaching extracurricular science to elementary school children on her lunch break. "We focused on making it fun, dynamic—filled with experiments and take-home projects for the kids," she explains.

At the start of her second year at the university, Keely met the man she'd marry. Together they moved to Vancouver so he could attend film school there. Conveniently, Mad Science had a Vancouver branch. Eventually Keely left Mad Science to work as an interpreter for both the H. R. MacMillan Space Center and the Vancouver Aquarium. This kind of interpreter doesn't translate foreign languages; instead, the job is like an informal educator, ready to answer questions, give a talk, or run a demonstration to enhance the visitors' experience.

It was at the aquarium where she came face-to-face with an octopus for the first time—a giant Pacific octopus, who utterly captivated her. "From that point on, I was hooked," she remembers. She learned everything she could about these smart, shape-shifting giants. Soon she was even able to witness—and help with—a thrilling but potentially risky new event at the aquarium: putting its male octopus, Clove, and its female, C.C., together.

Keely arrived early that morning because she didn't want to miss a thing. Clove was captured from his tank and moved in a transport bag to C.C.'s tank. Almost the moment he was released, the two octopuses embraced—and mated. Keely helped to make sure the event was caught on film.

Eleven months later, three hundred of their eggs hatched at the aquarium.

Unfortunately, none of Keely's octo hatchlings survived. Sad, but not unexpected—only one baby giant Pacific octopus (from Seattle) had previously survived to maturity in an aquarium. But the babies did provide aquarists with data that might one day help captive-born baby giant Pacific octopuses survive in captivity—perhaps for later release in the wild.

To the left of the octopus's eye, you can see the gill slit or mantle opening flung wide as the octopus inhales water to breathe. There is one gill slit on each side of the mantle.

AN OCTET OF OCTO FACTS

1. The seas are home to more than 250 species of octopus—ranging from the largest, the cold-water-loving giant Pacific, which may stretch longer than a limousine, to the tiniest, *Octopus wolfi*, which grows to only a half inch and lives in the warm Indo-Pacific. **THEY INCLUDE OCTOS WHO SPORT "EARS" LIKE DUMBO** (they're really fins), octos who glow in the dark (they live in the depths of the ocean), and others who are completely see-through.

2. The plural of *octopus* is not *octopi*. Though many people still use this plural, octopus experts deem it incorrect because it mixes up two languages. **OCTOPUS IS A GREEK WORD MEANING "EIGHT-FOOTED."** Adding *i* to the end of a singular noun is a Latin practice. The correct plural is *octopuses*, or *octopods*.

3. **AN OCTOPUS HAS THREE HEARTS.** In addition to a central heart, two others help pump blood at the base of each gill. The brain is unusual too. It's wrapped around the throat—and three-fifths of the nerve cells, or neurons (*NURE*-ons), that we normally associate with the brain are not there, but in the arms.

4. **THE OCTOPUS'S BLOOD ISN'T RED LIKE OURS, BUT BLUE.** Hemoglobin, the iron-based protein that carries oxygen to our cells, turns red when full of oxygen. But octopus blood has hemocyanin instead of hemoglobin, with copper binding to oxygen instead of iron—and copper turns octopuses' blood blue. Because copper isn't as efficient a carrier of oxygen as iron, octopuses tire rather quickly.

5. If a predator bites off an octopus's arm, **THE OCTOPUS CAN REGROW IT.** Meanwhile, if a severed arm escapes, it continues to thrash around, attracting predators away from the escaping animal.

6. Octopuses are members of one of the most successful groups of animals on earth—**THE MOLLUSKS**—which also includes mussels, clams, scallops, and snails, among others. Mollusks comprise one-quarter of the species in the sea. Within this broad classification, or phylum, octopuses belong to a smaller group, or class, called cephalopods (SEF-a-low-pods), which means "head-foot," because their limbs attach directly to their heads (an arrangement that means you find the octopus's mouth in its armpits). Most people think the octopus's rounded mantle (containing hearts, stomach, gills etc.) is its head, but no! The octopus's body isn't arranged like ours at all. The head-foot group also includes squids, cuttlefish, and the beautiful spiral-shelled nautiluses.

7. **OCTOPUSES LIVE FAST AND DIE YOUNG.** The longest-lived species of octopus, the giant Pacific, survives a scant three to five years. But the giant accomplishes a lot in this short time: hatching from an egg the size of a grain of rice, it can grow to eighty-eight pounds in its first year, making it one of the fastest-growing animals on earth.

8. **AN OCTOPUS CAN TASTE WITH ITS SKIN**—including its eyelids—but the sense is most exquisitely developed in the hundreds of suckers (the giant Pacific has 1,600 of them) on the underside of the arms. Each sucker can also act like a human's thumb and forefinger to delicately pick up small objects. And if one of those items tastes good, the octopus can pass the food from sucker to sucker to the mouth—like a conveyor belt.

CHAPTER 2

"What do we want? Number one, we want octopuses!" Jennifer told Yannick Chancerelle. He's the ginger-haired chief of scientific studies at CRIOBE, which stands for Centre de Researches Insulaires et Observatoire de l'Environnement de Polynésie Française (Center for Island Research and Observatory of the French Polynesian Environment), the research facility where we're staying.

We need Yannick's help to find our quarry, so Jennifer asked him about good study areas before we got started.

"Number two," she continued, "we want two different study locations—a complex environment with greater species richness, and a simpler one, so we can compare them. And we want to search close to the shore."

"That's going to be fringing reef," Yannick explained, mentioning one of the three main types of coral reefs scientists study. A fringing reef is found in shallow water near the shore. A barrier reef is separated from the shore by deep water; another coral reef type is an atoll, shaped like a ring with water in the middle.

Yannick had four suggestions right away—all of them within a fifteen-minute drive of our base. That was lucky, since CRIOBE has only three vehicles and two boats to share among its residents, which this July include a dozen French university students as well as us. Two of the vehicles are aging Mitsubishi L200 pickup trucks, meant to seat only two—three if the skinniest person squeezes in between the passenger seat and the stick shift. The third is what we dub the Frankencar. It used to be a four-door Peugeot 205, but now has only one working door and a trunk and back modified to carry scuba, snorkeling, and scientific gear. So much of its original body has been replaced with pieces of other vehicles that it reminds us of Mary Shelley's famous monster.

One of the sites Yannick recommended is by a white sand beach dotted with coconut trees owned by a church, so we call the site Church Copse. We can see a cardinal marker, a buoy to help pilots navigate safely, in the distance. Another is near a picnic area, where the water turns from turquoise to steely blue about three thousand feet from shore at a steep drop-off. A third site is near a distinctive palm that grows horizontally, and we call it Bent Palm. The fourth is just past a marina—the place where Jennifer found the shell and David found the crab parts yesterday.

So today, we plan to scout some of the other sites Yannick recommended. David drives Tatiana and me to the picnic site, and then drives back to CRIOBE to get Jennifer.

It's a gorgeous sunny day, 88 degrees. Palm trees wave in the tropical breeze. For breakfast, we enjoyed bananas and papaya we bought by the side of the road. Tatiana and I wade expectantly into the clear shallows of paradise.

Quickly, we see we are not alone. Looking down, we discover that lying on the white sand near our feet are dozens—no, hundreds—wait, thousands!—of fat, tube-shaped creatures with thick, leathery skin. Each is fatter than a banana, and at least as long. Some are black. Some are dark burgundy with orange spots. Others are light gray, and still others light purple with dark spots. Yet more are brownish and almost look plaid. Double rows of suctioning tube feet hold them to the sand, and feathery tentacles at the other end wave like flags at the prow of a ship. Some seem to have little bumps all over their body, like a pickle.

"Sea cucumbers!" cries Tatiana admiringly. "This is very great!"

Turns out that what look like psychedelic overgrown zucchinis are gentle, surprising, and vitally important animals. Lying like vegetables on the bottom of the sea, these relatives of starfish and sand dollars seem helpless, but they have a startling method of defense: they can squirt their sticky digestive-system organs out of their anus. That's alarming enough to make any predator leave. Happily, the lucky sea cucumbers can regrow their insides later.

Sea cucumbers act as sea floor janitors. They take in sand through their front end, digesting any detritus, and send clean sand out the other end. Doing so fluffs up the sand, bringing needed oxygen, dissolved in the water, to all sorts of other creatures who live there—most of whom we can't see. "The biodiversity of the sand is so big, you wouldn't believe it," Tatiana says. Beneath our feet, worms, clams, and thousands of microscopic animals live in the sand—even in the spaces between individual sand grains, she explains. And they all depend on the sea cucumber. "The sea cucumber must be the most important oxygenator here," she says.

There's only one problem, says Tatiana: "If octopuses don't eat sea cucumbers"—and they don't—"then this is not the place for our study."

Careful not to step on the animals on the bottom, we don our fins and start swimming in the shallow water, our bellies just a foot or two from the sea floor. But everywhere we look, we find nothing but sand and sea cucumbers. There's no place for an octopus to den. There's nothing for an octopus to eat. "It's Sea Cucumber World!" says Tatiana.

So when Jennifer and David show up in the car, we decide to try another site, about two miles away—the area we call Church Copse.

Almost immediately, David spots crab remains. He rolls a rock away. "Do you see anything like an octopus underneath?" he asks Jennifer. Nada. "If there was an octopus here," says Jennifer, "it's gone now. Let's move on."

We swim, slowly scanning the bottom through our masks, breathing noisily through our snorkels. It's hard not to gasp at the beauty. Jennifer points out some of her favorite sea

The sea cucumber: an animal, not a vegetable.

Blacktip reef sharks. Beneath them, a stingray.

creatures, the butterfly fish. Named for beautiful colors and patterns as varied as butterflies', they come in orange, silver, red, white, fawn, spotted, and striped. The dozen or so species that live here all have a flat, disk-shaped body and pointy lips, as if waiting for a kiss. Maybe they are: butterfly fish are almost always found in pairs, as they mate for life.

Jennifer spots a large top shell, spiral and conical, the size of a giant grapefruit. "This is almost an ideal home for a young octopus," she tells me. "Let's hold it up and see if anyone comes walking out!"

Shells like these, originally secreted by a marine snail, later become home for all sorts of other creatures, from octopuses to hermit crabs. But when Jennifer holds it up, out comes nothing but sand and water. Anyone who called this shell home is out, outgrew it, or got eaten.

We swim to another steep drop-off, like the one we saw at the picnic area where the sea changes from a deep sky blue to vibrant turquoise. "You do the face," Jennifer says to David, sending him to deeper water where the reef forms a shallow cliff. "I'll do the flat." On one of her first dives, Jennifer turns up a two-inch orange crab carapace, intact and clean inside. Meanwhile, David pulls his head from the water to announce he's found something else.

"SHARK!" he calls. But David's not worried.

15

Giant clam.

The afternoon's swim is just as thrilling—and just as disappointing. Reddish-pink hogfish root in the sand for crustaceans. These fish start out female and later, triggered by hormones, become male. Bluestreak cleaner wrasses await "clients" at a coral landmark. These small, slender fish live off the parasites and dead skin of larger fish, who flock to special "cleaning stations" like clients to a hairdresser or spa. The big fish even let the cleaners go inside their mouth to do the job. A round, spotted toby looks at us with an expression like that of a surprised baby. It's not scared of us. If it were, it would inflate itself to more than twice its size by swallowing water and become too big for predators to swallow.

The shallows are full of dreamlike wonders. But we find no octopuses.

Dinner consists of a shiny blue fish called ature that some of our student friends bought for us at the side of the road, and which Jennifer fried in the CRIOBE kitchen and served with rice and salad. During the meal we discuss the day.

"Okay, so we didn't find them where we wanted to find them," Jennifer says. "So we have to decide: Where should we go tomorrow to look?"

I was beginning to wonder how anyone could *ever* find octopuses anywhere. The octopus specializes in looking like anything but itself. It squeezes itself into a den so tight you might

It's a four-foot blacktip reef shark, so named because each gray fin is distinctively tipped in ebony. Common to reefs in the Pacific and Indian Oceans, this species is usually timid around people, and would much rather munch on a fish—or an octopus—than on one of us. It takes one look at David and me and turns away, its movements as graceful and fluid as water itself.

David dives again and soon spots something even more interesting—crab remains. "Ooooooh!" he says through his snorkel. He collects them in his bucket.

We swim for two hours, reveling in strangeness and beauty. Fish fly by like birds. Others seem to float like lazy balloons. And still more animals peek at us from among the living and dead coral: baby fish, who use the coral crevices as a nursery; black sea urchins, whose spines contain poison; giant clams, with what look like crooked smiles with iridescent lips—which they purse in fear upon our approach. (The clams seem misnamed, as those whom we see are only slightly larger than our fists. This is the smallest of several species of giant clams—the largest can grow to five hundred pounds, making them the heaviest mollusks on the planet.)

Church Copse, with its strong current, brings more nutrients and offers a more varied habitat than Sea Cucumber World. "This area is so different from the first site," says Jennifer. "It looks so good—but we're not seeing anybody yet."

never see it there, hides or rests most of the time, and moves dens frequently. How do you find a hiding, invisible creature in a place you've never been to before?

Each scientist uses a slightly different method. Tatiana has a good eye for what a den looks like, says Jennifer. Tatiana explains: "In this kind of reef, we need to look for a difference in the substrate"— something different along the bottom that gives the octopus an inspiration for camouflage or a place to hide—"a rock on the sand, or a hole in the coral."

Jennifer, on the other hand, looks for piles of intact shells. Such "garbage heaps" are known as middens, she explains, and she considers these the best giveaway that an octopus is occupying a home nearby.

David has found hundreds of giant Pacific octopuses in Alaska's frigid waters. But none of them was visible in its den. He finds them by probing the den with a long green alder stick, which the octopus grabs and tugs. "I've never found *this* species," he admits, "and never seen an octopus in a den. I'm not used to coral reefs." But he's never failed to find octopus dens. Ever.

We pore over the map and discuss our options.

"Maybe we'd get better water clarity if we searched the lagoons," suggests David.

"What about looking under the dock?" asks Jennifer.

Perhaps, offers Keith, we should hire a fisherman to show us where to find them.

"Tatiana has more experience than I do in areas like this," says David. "Do you think," he asks her, "we should go back and search again where we've already gone to?"

Tatiana thinks it's worth another try. "It's normal for this to take a few days," she says. "We need to find our eyes. We've only just started. It's a camouflaged animal—it's hard to find."

"The octopuses are there," agrees Jennifer. "Who else takes the claws of crabs and piles them upside down inside shells? And besides," she adds, "when you go into the field—as we all know—you know what you want to do, but it doesn't always happen that way. The laboratory is about control—but the field is about serendipity."

Nobody expected to find octopuses the first day of looking. And it might have been too much to hope to find one the second day, either. But we're here for only a limited amount of time—I have to leave in two weeks, for instance—and finding the first octopus is only step one of the study. Tomorrow will be our third day. Jennifer can tell I'm getting nervous.

In our shared room that night, after we have both tucked in our mosquito nets and turned out the light, Jennifer's voice comes, soft but assertive, in the dark:

"We know what we're looking for," she tells me, "but we don't know how long it will take. We'll find octopuses. I don't know how many. I don't know how good the data will be . . .

"But we'll find octopuses, know that. We've got bloodhounds! My team is really good."

A pod of dolphins is a frequent sight in the waters of Moorea.

CRIOBE

With its sophisticated laboratories, extensive library, comprehensive collections room, dive center, kitchen, and dorms, CRIOBE's field station has stood at the forefront of coral reef research for four decades, attracting students from France (of which French Polynesia is a part) and researchers from around the world.

One reason Moorea is a hotbed of research is that the reefs here were relatively undisturbed until the 1980s. Then came a series of disasters, some natural and some man-made. A plague of reef-eating starfish invaded in 1980 and '81; hurricanes and cyclones struck the island for the first time since 1906 in 1982, and then again in 1991; and the human population of the island increased threefold between 1971 and 1996. These changes made Moorea's previously pristine reefs an even more valuable living laboratory, allowing researchers to study how reefs respond to such threats—events that endanger coral reefs worldwide as human numbers swell and change the earth's climate.

CRIOBE grew from France's earliest studies of coral reef ecosystems, back in the 1960s. As a joint project of France's National Museum of Natural History and its High School for Practical Studies, CRIOBE archives the data on coral reefs stretching back in time longer than any other institution in the entire Pacific Ocean. An earlier field station was located along Cook's Bay in 1971; CRIOBE's current campus was built on Opunohu Bay in 1981.

At CRIOBE, graduate students study the nesting success of endangered sea turtles, count and classify creatures as diverse as fire corals and sea cucumbers, and compare the results of surveys with the first studies done on Moorea in 1971. Researchers dispatched from CRIOBE study the sea life of other French Polynesian islands as well—and even discover new species. A pufferfish new to science was described by an American-French collaboration in 2012. The new species was named *Canthigaster criobe* in the institution's honor.

The CRIOBE campus.

Vanessa Conrad, a student, studies giant clams.

Franck Lerouvreur, dive operator.

Pauline Bosserelle, left, and Claire Bonneville conduct water surveys as part of their research at CRIOBE.

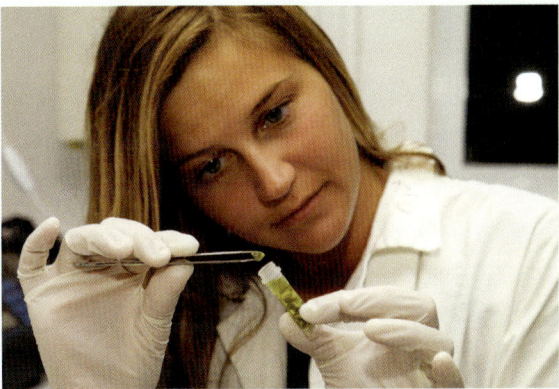
Caroline Dube, working topside, explores the genetics of fire coral in the lab.

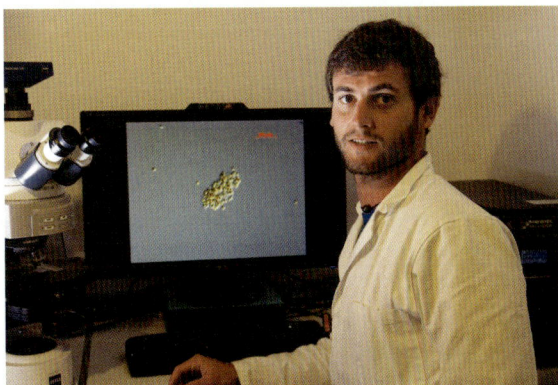
Alexandre Merciere uses the microscope to study coral growth.

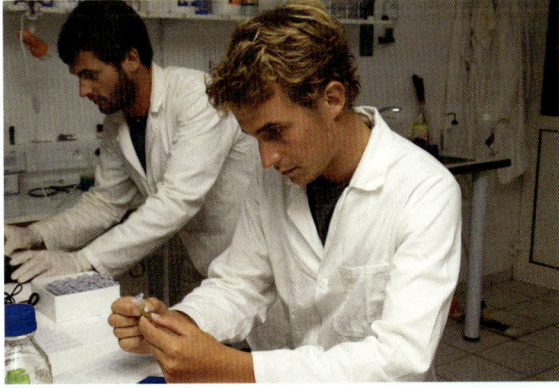
Research student Marc Besson labels fire coral samples.

CHAPTER 3

Wet bathing suits. Wet scuba booties. Wet wetsuits. In French Polynesia, it's winter in July. When we're donning wet gear in the morning, even temperatures below 70 feel downright chilly. David calls it "the wet kiss of anticipation—of getting in the water and finding an octopus!"

We worked out our plan the night before. We're heading back to Church Copse to explore an area with numerous gullies and both live and dead coral—the sort of place where Jennifer and Tatiana have seen octopuses in their previous studies at other tropical sites. They will work the shallows while David and I head to deeper waters.

We walk into the shallows, don our fins, masks, and snorkels, and start swimming. A brisk ten-minute swim takes David and me past the shallows to where finally the water is over our heads. "Now we look for octopus!" he says—and then dives like a seal.

I follow him and discover a whole different world. Corals flecked with blue and yellow. Fish with iridescent stripes and glowing eyes. Fish with black masks like bandits, and fish with orange bellies that glow like fire. Many look more like modern sculptures than something alive. Some of Jennifer's favorites, Moorish idols, are dressed more flamboyantly than rock stars, in bold stripes of yellow, black, and white. From the back of the head, slender white dorsal fins trail beyond their tails like banners in a breeze.

When David emerges from his dive, I can hear his spout even though I'm underwater. I surface and tread water to see what he's found: two crab claws piled on a flame scallop shell, like a stack of plates piled in the kitchen sink after dinner. "A den, but no octopus," he says. "But I declare this site very promising."

We continue our exploration. We spot a handsome reddish hawkfish. A loner with a large head and thick body, it watches us from atop a yellowish coral. Thanks to the large pectoral fins on the sides of their bodies, these fish are capable of perching safely even on stinging fire coral—a species that, happily, we haven't yet encountered. Pairs of mated butterfly fish with dazzling stripes swim by us like proud couples in an Easter parade.

David returns from one dive holding more clam shells—possible remains of octo meals—and drops them into the collecting bucket on his weight belt and fastens the lid. We return to cruising along the surface, scanning below the way pilots of low-flying aircraft look down on a city. Once you get over the dazzle and shimmer

This stingray measured more than five feet across.

of their colors, you can watch the fish for what they are doing: darting into corals, peeking out of hiding holes, hurrying along on their way like busy people in New York City. And they are probably doing basically the same things as people: looking for suitable food and mates and homes, and trying to stay safe while they go about their daily chores.

A loose school of small black fish with white side stripes contracts into a tight ball as David dives again. He emerges with more shells—the bounty of a detective at work on a whodunit, trying to locate the perpetrator with clues supplied by the victims.

We reach the cardinal marker by ten a.m. With a shallow dive, we inspect beneath the cement piling and see it's encrusted with young yellow and orange coral. "You just know an octopus sat here and enjoyed its morning tea," David says. "It's too beautiful a spot to pass up." The animal could easily change its skin to rest here in complete invisibility.

A hawksbill sea turtle swims by, oaring the water with its winglike, leathery front flippers, each with one distinctive claw sticking out like a thumb on a mitten. The species is critically endangered, mainly because people eat its eggs. Unlike the turtle, though, I am not going forward—but backwards. When I pause, treading water, to take notes in pencil on my white plastic underwater dive slate, I look up to see that the current has carried me far from David. "Don't drift out to sea while you write!" he shouts.

Once I catch up, we round the point together. We continue our octopus search on our way back to join Tatiana and Jennifer in the shallows.

David dives, picks up rocks, shines his underwater flashlight into crevices. He's finding plenty of evidence that octopuses live here: beside little caves in dead coral, shells are stacked up one atop the other, with crab claws resting on top, like spoons in a bowl. "Nobody else is going to leave these in a pile!" he says. "The octopus must have just stepped out." He's found more than ten separate piles of food remains, so many that he's stopped collecting them in his bucket, and at least three potential octopus homes. And he keeps looking—even inside a green glass bottle, in case a youngster's hiding there. Back in the States, off the Pacific Northwest coast, a small species known as the red octopus favors beer bottles as homes, especially stubby brown ones. But nobody's home in ours.

We see that the sky overhead is bruised with dark clouds. A storm is gathering. So we turn toward shore to look for Jennifer and Tatiana. There they are! We wave—and they wave back

The hawksbill sea turtle is endangered worldwide.

An octopus peers at us from atop some coral.

enthusiastically. Only once we're within a hundred yards can we hear what they're shouting at us. "OCTOPUS!"

It's 10:10 by the time we catch up. Jennifer pulls her head out of the water just long enough to say "Mmmmnnthth!" She's so excited, she forgets to pull her snorkel out of her mouth at first. Seeing our puzzled expressions, she remembers to remove it. "I'm looking at an octopus!" she says, then pops the snorkel back in and plunges below again.

By the time I can locate it, the octopus has retreated into a hole. All I can see are white suckers along one bluish arm, curved inside a small cavern in some dead coral. Jennifer announces that she will name it Kwila after her dog, a half malamute, half border collie she adopted as a puppy.

It turns out Kwila is the second octopus of the day! Tatiana was the first to spot one—and she found it during the first ten minutes of their foray. It was hunting, spread across a shallow gully, its skin a beautiful blue-green color. "When it saw me, its head turned brown, and then its arms turned brown," she says, "and then it went down its hole." She named it Cleo, after her white poodle—a dog who has no fewer than three octopus-shaped plush toys to play with.

The clouds that were gathering are now hissing down rain. It's cold above water, but from beneath the surface, looking up, the drops look like inside-out dimples and the rain sounds like sizzling grease. Jennifer asks us to make just a few more passes over the shallows. "Look for disruption. Somebody moving rubble around." We agree to turn back at eleven—water is not a good place to be when there might be lightning. We all head toward shore.

The team is confident now. "As soon as we got here," says Tatiana, "I said, 'Yeah! This is the place. We've found our study area!'" Our site reminds her of one of her octopus study areas in Brazil, Tatiana tells us as she sits down in the foot-deep water to remove her fins and walk ashore. David takes one last look—and right beside Tatiana he finds a pile of shells, a hole in the rock—and inside, another octopus! Sticking with the dog theme, he names it Grover, after the beagle his family adopted when he was ten.

Before leaving, we mark the three dens so we can find them again. We leave a collection bucket tied to a rock near one and a red bungee cord at another. We haul a flat black rock over to mark the third. In the cold rain, we pile into the truck to return to CRIOBE, wash our gear, and take a hot shower. It doesn't matter that nobody has a dry towel.

HOW SMART IS AN OCTOPUS?

Measuring the minds of other creatures is a perplexing problem. One yardstick scientists use is brain size—because humans have such big brains. But size doesn't always matter. Think of computers: the first ones were as big as rooms; now they fit in your pocket.

Still, octopuses have the largest brains of any invertebrate. A giant Pacific octopus's brain is about the size of a parrot's. That's only as big as a walnut, but scientists now know that a walnut-size brain is enough to allow at least some parrots to add numbers, make jokes, and invent new words.

As another measure of intelligence, scientists count nerve cells, or neurons. A human brain has 100 billion neurons. The common octopus (the only octopus species in which anyone has counted neurons) has 130 million in its brain and almost 200 million, or three-fifths of its total neurons, in its arms. As the philosopher-diver Peter Godfrey-Smith observed, "It is as if each arm has a mind of its own."

Perhaps the most convincing evidence of octopus intelligence comes from what they do—in the wild, in aquariums, and in the laboratory. Octopuses learn new skills fast, and remember what they learn. "We know from many studies that octopuses are smart," says Jennifer. With her Seattle colleague Roland Anderson and others, Jennifer has conducted many of these studies herself. One study showed that octopuses learn and remember individual human faces. One set of volunteers fed captive octopuses fish and squid. Another set, dressed identically, touched the octopuses with a bristly stick, which octopuses don't like. The octopuses quickly learned to approach the people who fed them even when those people had no food. But when they saw the people who had touched them with the bristly stick, the octopuses moved away—or blasted those people with salt water from their funnels!

In the wild, octopuses have to solve different kinds of problems all the time. *How can I safely capture that spiny crab? How can I escape that hungry moray eel? What can I collect from my travels to make this coral crevice into a safe den?* (Some octopuses in the wild have been filmed carrying coconut halves to use as portable huts; others use shells as doors to their lairs.) In captivity, they quickly figure out solutions too, such as how to open a container when there's a tasty food item inside.

At the New England Aquarium in Boston, to keep the octopuses entertained, Wilson Menashi, an engineer, designed an elaborate set of three clear plastic cubes, each with a different kind of latch on the lid. Once the octopus, inspired by the prospect of eating a tasty crab inside, learned to master opening the first cube, Menashi next placed the first cube within a second cube—and then both of those inside a third with *two* different locks: a bolt that slides into position, and a lever arm like on a canning jar. Most of the dozen octopuses Menashi has known over nearly two decades have learned to open all three boxes within a few minutes, after just a handful of once-a-week tries.

But octopuses are individuals, and some are smarter than others. Some come up with solutions to problems that researchers don't anticipate. One eager female octo at the New England Aquarium, Gwenevere, didn't bother with the latches and just crushed the box. She created a small hole through which she grabbed the crab. Another octopus also skipped the latches. He got so excited when he saw the crab, he poured his whole body through the hole Gwenevere had created. Visitors found him squeezed into a perfect cube shape in his exhibit—an octopus-in-the-box.

A meeting of the minds: an octopus sizes up a coral grouper.

25

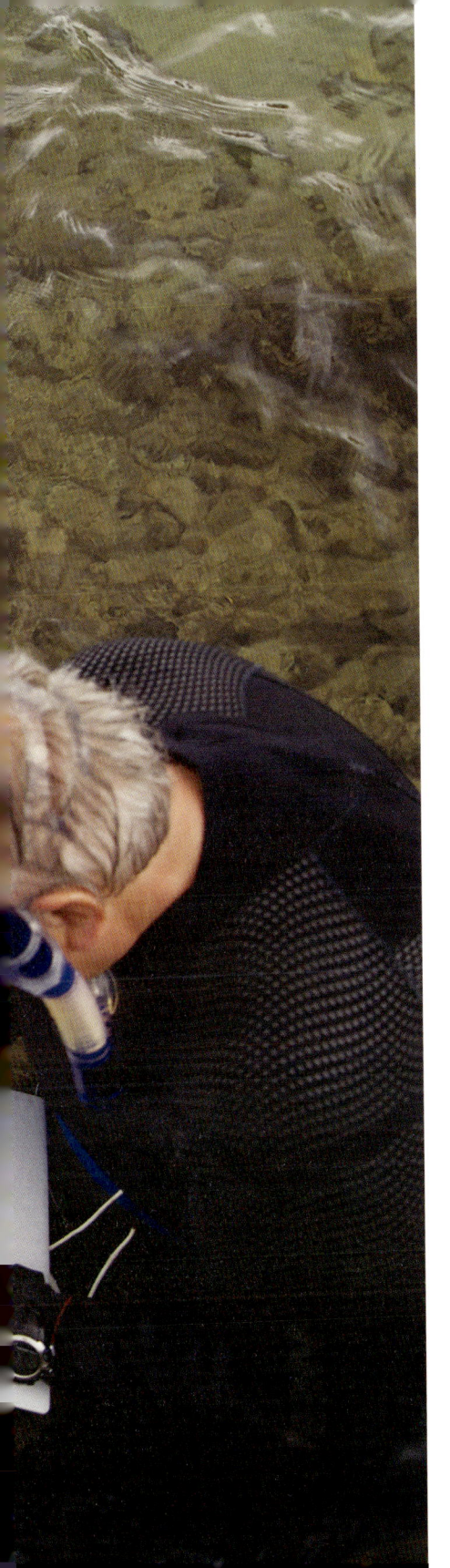

CHAPTER 4

"We have been lucky and smart!" Jennifer congratulates us at a meeting convened after lunch. "We have found a place with three octopuses and think there are many more. We've found our first study location!"

And just in time, Keely Langford, from the Vancouver Aquarium, has joined us. A competitive swimmer, she dives regularly in the aquarium's large tanks and is used to finding hiding sea animals. She's brought with her the equipment we'll need: a bouquet of three-inch orange buoys that we can tie with rope to mark our octopus dens so we can return to them for our study, more dive slates on which to take notes, and collection buckets for the prey we discover outside the dens, so we can take them back to CRIOBE's lab for identification.

Soon we can begin taking data. Jennifer reviews the protocol, the procedure we'll follow every time. First, check the den to see if the octopus is in. If so, administer the personality test. What does the octopus do as we approach it? Hide? Change color? Squirt ink? Or come out? Next, gently touch the octopus with a pencil. What does it do? Does it leave the burrow? Block the entry? Grab the pencil? And finally, collect the prey remains around the den. What does the octopus do then? Does it erect papillae? Blow a jet of water? Just watch? Or ignore us completely? We'll take notes underwater by writing on our dive slates, and hope it doesn't rub off before we log the data. (But oddly, we discover the slates take some effort to clean. We debate whether toothpaste or tile cleaner works better to scrub them.)

Next, we'll survey the habitat around the octopus's den. We'll work along a transect, a fixed path along which we'll record what we find at regular intervals. One of us will stretch out a long, waterproof tape measure for twenty meters (scientists prefer the metric system—one meter is 3.2 feet) around the den in two randomly chosen directions. Every twenty centimeters (a centimeter is .39 inch) we look down and record what's below. David has created a checklist, printed on waterproof paper, and worked out a shorthand for recording what we find: RC means reef rock, we'll use SP for sponge, SD for sand, RB for rubble, and so on. Each checklist is labeled with the octopus's name, den depth, site name, and date.

And finally, once we get back to CRIOBE, all the octopus prey remains must be identified. Our work is cut out for us—and we can't wait to get back in the water.

A portrait of an octopus flaunting his jet (on your left, below the eye).

ful sweep of the tides. To steady ourselves, one hand is usually holding on to something on the bottom while the other is clutching equipment, leaving no way to adjust a flooded or steamy mask or pick up a shell or a rock.

Even with our earlier makeshift markers, we have trouble locating our octopus dens. One hole in coral rubble looks much like the next, and each patch of rubble offers so many holes. And when we eventually find them, there's not much to see. To our disappointment, Grover isn't home. Cleo is, but as we are in the process of locating her home, the octopus retreats so deep into her hole that it's no use doing the personality test. There is no sign of Kwila. And nobody finds any new octopus dens. We mark the unoccupied dens with our buoys, collect the prey remains, and head back for lunch.

The next day is a comedy of errors.

At low tide, the octopus dens are in such shallow water that it's almost impossible to swim. We have to frog-kick to move forward—there's not enough room to move our fins up and down without hitting the bottom, possibly injuring a sea animal and hopelessly clouding the water.

In many ways, deeper waters would be much safer, and would surely be more comfortable: here we are always at risk of puncture by the poisonous spines of sea urchins or the deadly and nearly invisible sand-colored stonefish. We're constantly scraping our fingers, knees, and bellies on the sharp skeletons of dead corals that poke up from the bottom. The ropes of our buoy markers and collection buckets and the lines holding our pencils to our dive slates tangle on the dead coral and one another. Our chins, foreheads, and lips plow into clots of large brown bristly algae called *Turbinaria ornata*. It feels like washing your face with a pinecone. And we're smack in the worst of the surge, the power-

At this point, I start making a list: "Why it's hard to work in a marine environment."

Everyone has something to add.

"Salt water is corrosive and wrecks your equipment," David offers. "It's not a matter of if but *when* your waterproof camera gets flooded."

"That's why we can't use many of the electronics that other researchers use on land," adds Jennifer.

"Then there's lack of air," notes David.

"A weird sunburn on your forehead, which stops at the top of your facemask," adds Keely.

This species of algae grows rapidly, detaching from the bottom to spread along the surface.

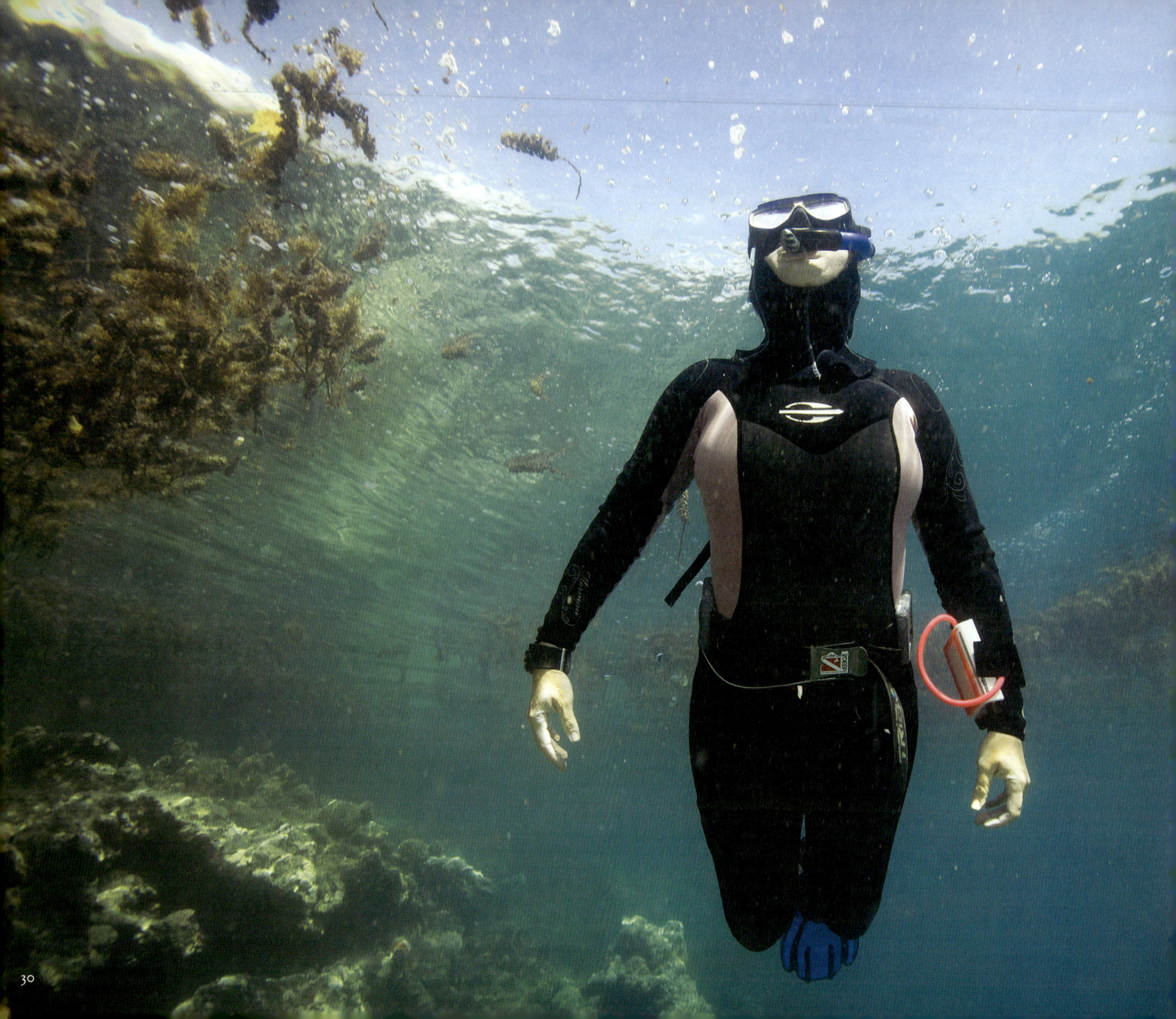

The list grows fast:

Human senses are distorted underwater. Smell is extinguished. With water in your ears, hearing is muffled—and because water is eight hundred times denser than air, sound waves move faster but sound direction is difficult to determine. Underwater, objects seem bigger and closer than they really are. (That's because underwater you need an air space between your eyes and the water for your eyes to focus, provided by your facemask. But light bends as it travels through this space, so things look 25 percent larger than in air.)

You get cold easily—that's because heat conducts away from the body twenty-five times faster in water than in air. The surge of the sea jostles you as you work. Everything is wet all the time—your hair, your towel, your equipment. Coral cuts your skin, and in the humid tropics, bacteria that cause infections thrive. Sun burns the tops of your ears, and if you have short hair, the back of your neck. Your dive mask pulls your hair . . .

Keely has an idea. "Let's make another list—of why it's *great* to work in a marine environment." This list is more fun to compile.

"You're in a whole new world," says Keely.

"You're weightless," adds Keith.

In the water, you're free of so many of the constraints and demands of the land, including its frenetic pace. "You cannot rush," says Tatiana. "You must do everything at the speed of the water. And I love the silence of the sea."

Best of all, everyone agrees, in the ocean, wildlife is all around you, in far greater densities and variety than in any imaginable experience on land.

And . . . octopuses live there!

Still, they are proving awfully hard to study.

MAKING FRIENDS WITH AN OCTOPUS

I have always loved watching octopuses in public aquariums, and had always dreamed of actually meeting one. In March of 2011, I got my chance.

At the New England Aquarium in Boston, one of the keepers took me behind the scenes. He opened the top of the tank housing the aquarium's giant Pacific octopus. Her name was Athena, he told me—and immediately, the octopus turned bright red with excitement and flowed over to meet me.

Athena's eye swiveled in its socket and locked on to my own. I plunged my arms into the cold 47-degree water, and her eight arms came boiling out, reaching for mine. She latched on to the skin of my arms and hands with her suckers, and soon I had the honor of feeling dozens of her strong, beautiful white suckers tasting me at once. They felt like cold, wet kisses with extra-strong suction.

I knew Athena was powerful enough to pull me into her tank, but I was never afraid. And she wasn't afraid of me, either. How did I know? Because Athena allowed me to stroke her head—the first time she had done this with a stranger. And her skin turned white beneath my touch. I later learned that this is the color of a relaxed giant Pacific octopus.

Our interaction lasted more than a quarter of an hour before she let go of me. Even though Athena and I last shared a common evolutionary ancestor 500 million years ago, I strongly felt she was as curious about me as I was about her. Across the chasm of half a billion years, it seemed we were having a meeting of the minds.

I visited Athena twice more after that. Alas, just as we were becoming friends, she died of old age—which for a giant Pacific octopus can be the tender age of three. But since her death, I've come to know four other giant Pacific octopuses at the New England Aquarium, all of them females. Each had her own distinct personality. Each came to know me, and would rise to the top of the tank to greet me and explore my skin with her suckers.

The spring that Athena died, I met her successor, Octavia. I visited her every week. At first she was shy. But soon she came to know me. When my friend Wilson Menashi (the man who designed the locking cubes to entertain the octopus) would open the tank, she would hurry to meet us, and then flip upside down to accept a fish from our hands. Sometimes she'd try to pull me in, or reach for my face, or hold my hands with her arms.

A year after we met, Octavia laid eggs, and her behavior changed. At night, when nobody could see her, she began attaching long chains of oval, cream-colored eggs, each one the size of a grain of rice, to the ceiling and sides of her lair. Her eggs were infertile because she had no mate, but she probably didn't know that. Now she wanted nothing to do with us. She occasionally accepted fish we handed her with a long tool, but for ten months, she was completely absorbed with her eggs, cleaning them, fluffing them, and guarding them.

Octopuses lay eggs only once, at the end of their lives, and Octavia was nearing the end of hers. The following spring, when her egg chains were disintegrating, Octavia developed an eye infection. Her keeper, Bill Murphy, decided to move Octavia to another tank behind the scenes, where her condition could be better monitored. A volunteer tried to urge her into a bucket, so she could be moved. Octavia wouldn't go. But when Bill, her best human friend, who had known her and fed her since the day she arrived at the aquarium, touched her, she immediately agreed to enter the bucket. She was then safely transferred into the other tank.

And when I came in to visit her in her new home, she floated right to the top of the tank, looked into my eyes, and embraced me with her suckers. Even though she had not touched or looked at me for ten months, even though she was very old and probably very tired and weak, she remembered me and made the effort to greet me one last time.

I can't know exactly what I meant to Octavia. But I know what she, and Athena, and the other octopuses I have known have meant to me. I am immensely grateful to them, for they have given me a great gift. They have given me a far deeper understanding of what it means to think and feel and know. They have shown me that, even though our lives could not be more different, an octopus and a person can find connection with each other.

An octopus uses the webbing between its arms to keep prey from getting away, throwing the webbing over the prey like a blanket to prevent escape.

34

CHAPTER 5

Preserved pufferfish. Former flounders. Ex-eels. As we sit at the table in CRIOBE's collections room each night, the specimens seem to stare down at us from where they float in formalin or coil in glass jars. They're perched atop tall wooden cases filled with 126 drawers of shells, crab carapaces, and small stoppered vials of marine creatures—a library filled not with books but with bodies. Tens of thousands of specimens surround us as we struggle with the giant jigsaw puzzle of figuring out what our octopuses ate—a puzzle with some of the pieces missing.

"That Cleo, she really ate!" David says. He's looking at a dozen items collected from her den. He selects just one to start.

"Would you agree," he asks Jennifer, "that this is a fragment of a cowrie shell?"

Normally a cowrie would be easy to identify: these shiny, egg-shaped shells, the former home of marine snails, sport slitlike openings on the bottom and beautiful designs on top. They're used for money in West Africa, as a badge of rank in Fiji, and a way to consult spirits and predict the future in India. The problem is, we've only got a *piece* of the shell—and it's all we've got to try to figure out which one of the twenty species of cowrie known to be in Moorea's waters (there are more than two hundred in the ocean) this one is.

"What we're doing here is very different detective work" from what we do in the water, Jennifer explains. "Identifying all these shells is an absorbing task." On the table in front of us are piles of books from CRIOBE's library, with titles such as *Shells of the Western Pacific in Color* and *Crustacea of New Caledonia*. Others are in French: *Les Récifs Coraliens de Tahiti et ses Îles*.

We're lucky with this cowrie. Even though it's just a fragment, the piece we have is part of its upper side, showing a milky blue oval ringed in orange. That's enough to instantly identify it as the ring cowrie, *Monetaria annulus*—one of the species used for money, and among the most

Scallop shells.

In CRIOBE's library, Keely consults a reference book.

widespread and best known of the cowries in the world.

Unfortunately, though, "we don't always have the diagnostic pattern in hand," Jennifer says. "And it can get really complicated!" For instance, consider the scallop shell Jennifer found outside Kwila's den: it looks like the one she found in one of her books. "This shell has ridges and looks like that one," Jennifer says, pointing to the picture. "*Mantellum fragilis kiliense*? Oh, no," she says, reading further. "That's supposed to be Japanese . . ."

Meanwhile, David is looking up crab species in a different volume. "There's a thousand species of crustaceans here!" he says in amazement.

How do you even start on such a big project? Jennifer explains: "First, we try to get the big shape—and get to the family." This doesn't mean we want to meet the crab's bereaved parents; "family" is a broad scientific classification of related animals, all of whom share certain physical characteristics. For instance, all cats—from your housecat to a lion—are in the same family, Felidae. All cats have short snouts, shearing teeth, and legs adapted for running.

Jennifer and David are looking at a crab carapace that was left outside Cleo's den. The hindmost pair of legs on all crabs in this family are paddlelike—which helps them swim. That places them within the family Thalamita, known as the swimming crabs. Now they can try to narrow things down further—to genus and species. If you were trying to classify a cat, you might ask if it has the special bone in the throat called the hyoid. If so, you'd know your cat belongs to the genus Panthera, the roaring cats: tigers, leopards, jaguars, and lions. And next you might ask: Does it have a mane? Then it's a lion, *Panthera leo*. Stripes? A tiger, *Panthera tigris*. And so on.

For crabs, the process is the same. Every detail must be scrutinized. "We need to look carefully," says Jennifer, "and ask ourselves: What is the shape of the carapace? What about the claws? Are there spines on them?" It might be the clue to classifying the creature within a smaller group, and then a smaller one yet, and finally determining the species.

"Notice the particular shape these claws have," Jennifer says to David. "Is it *Thalamita chaptalii*?" That one has triangular bumps on the carapace. Or *Thalamita crenata*? That one has blue and red on the claws. Or could it be *Thalamita integra*, with red lines across the claws . . . ?

As frustrating as it sometimes seems, we're making important progress—and having fun, too. "Oh, wow! We have three unknown crabs here, gang," David announces. They're not in the books. Maybe they are in the specimen drawers. Who knows—maybe we will discover a new species, or find a known species in a place

David displays a crab carapace.

where it's never been recorded before.

"I'm a jigsaw puzzle fanatic," says Jennifer. "This is what I do when I can't be watching the animal behave."

Jennifer and David work late into the night. The rest of us head for bed, hoping to dream of octopuses—and to actually find some the next day.

For most of our first week, it's been two steps forward and one step back—promise and revelation, then disappointment. True, we're making progress. But it's been punctuated with frustration.

While the rest of the team was still scouting sites, Keith went scuba diving with CRIOBE's divemaster, Franck Lerouvreur, along the barrier reef to the east of Opunohu Bay—and spotted an octopus hiding in its home! The next day, Keith returned to the site. To his astonishment, the octopus let him stick around as it roamed, changing color and pattern while traveling over roughly a fifty-square-foot area of reef, for more than half an hour. "It was like this dude was showing me around," Keith said in wonder. "He seemed playful, and not afraid at all." At one point the octopus even met up with another octopus. While Keith was photographing the first octopus, the second one stood up tall on its arms as if to get a better look, peering at the scene with what seemed

Following an octopus, Keith met a second one.

like keen interest. "In all my years photographing animals underwater—sharks, tuna, turtles, fish—I've never encountered anything that watched me like this—like watching a model at a fashion photo shoot, or watching a pro football player at a game. Most of the time fish observe you and notice you. They don't appear to watch and learn. It was incredible!" Keith said.

Keith got fabulous photos, and the next day took me scuba diving with him to find the octopus again. We saw dolphins skipping over the surface like stones. We met eight blacktip reef sharks swimming together like dogs running in a pack. But the octopus was gone, unavailable for study, and was not seen again for the rest of our trip.

Back in the shallows, Tatiana and David began habitat transects at Church Copse, yielding three hundred valuable pieces of data from the areas around each den. We all continued to collect shell remains, resulting in a growing menu of octo food items. Jennifer completed the personality test on Cleo (shy) and Grover (bolder).

Sometimes we couldn't even find the octopuses in our marked dens. One day we took Yannick's two children, Tamatea, age seven, and Vaimiti, eleven, with us to Church Copse to show them our study subjects. Maybe they could help us find more. Both kids learned how to swim at age three and are almost as at home in the sea as on land. But none of the resident octopuses was in its den. And we found no new octopuses.

The second octopus stood up tall to watch Keith photograph the first.

Jennifer with Tamatea and Vaimiti.

Equally worrisome, we need at least one other site—or there will be nothing with which to compare the first one, a crucial element in the study.

Just short of the end of our first week in Moorea, Tatiana and David return from a provisioning trip to one of the small grocery stores. They've brought baguettes, cereal, lettuce, tomatoes, cheese, frozen vegetables—and two crab carapaces, the shells of one limpet and one cowrie. "From our new site!" David announces triumphantly. On their way back from the store, he and Tatiana scouted another shallow area on the other side of the bay, a welcome contrast to Church Copse: with a sandy, easy approach, it has more live coral and less of the annoying *Turbinaria ornata* algae. It's a quick twenty-minute drive away, close to a dive shop. It even has a picnic table for lunch.

But does it have octopuses?

We're eager to find out, though today our first priority is to return to Church Copse to complete the transects. While there, of course, we'll look for prey remains—and more octopuses.

Hours pass and we find no new study animals. Tatiana begins the process of ferrying people back to CRIOBE in one of the pickups. Keith and I return first. Tatiana turns back for Jennifer. David and Keely will stay longest, since they can come back in the Frankencar.

David is working on the third transect when Keely, snorkeling fifty yards away, sees something move among the rubble. Could it be an octopus? How to find out? *Should I touch it?* she wonders, and reaches out her hand . . . then sees it's not an octopus at all. It's another master of disguise, who looks exactly like a rock. A poisonous stonefish.

Whew! Gotta be careful, Keely thinks. Shaken, she turns to swim toward David. On her way, another slight movement catches her eye. She's sure this time: That *one's an octopus!*

A mottled brown, the animal pokes its head out of its den and looks Keely square in the eye. Is it Kwila? Or someone new? Because octopuses change color and shape, no one can tell for sure. As Jennifer continues to look for more octopuses, Keely administers the personality test. The animal watches her closely. But when she touches it, the animal retreats into its den. Whoever it is, it's a rather shy octopus.

Tatiana returns to collect Jennifer, leaving David and Keely to finish the new transect. At CRIOBE, Keith sorts his photos, Tatiana catalogs the transect data, and Jennifer and I start cooking dinner. Before we know it, it's five thirty p.m.—then six—then six fifteen . . . and getting dark. "What's keeping them?" asks Jennifer.

Though she remains calm, our expedition leader is nervous. The ocean can be dangerous even in the shallows. She knows these waters are home to deadly stonefish, and hopes our friends haven't run into one. Spines along its back inject a venom powerful enough to kill a person and is so painful that victims have been known to demand the affected limb be cut off.

It's six thirty when Keely staggers, exhausted, into the kitchen—sodden but excited. As David hoses the salt water from the back of the Frankencar, Keely tells us what happened:

"Right after Tatiana picked up Jennifer," she says, "I start to swim toward David—and I see this rock outcropping with shells on a shelf! Here's definitely the best midden we've seen." She counted seventeen food items in all, mostly crab parts, all tucked carefully into a small crevice to the left and below a hole in the rock. She free-dived and looked in . . . "and there's the octopus sitting inside, with arms curled into the shape of a handlebar mustache, looking right at me!"

She's sure it's none of the other animals from Church Copse. Size is hard to judge in an octopus, but she's certain that the distance between this one's eyes is much smaller than in the others.

When David surfaced from his transect, expecting the long day was done, Keely was almost afraid to tell him they now had another transect to do, plus the personality test and prey collection. But David was thrilled—and so were we!

HOW OCTOPUSES CHANGE COLOR

Octopuses put chameleons to shame. An octopus can change its entire appearance—going from red to white, from stripes to spots, from bumpy to smooth—in one-tenth of a second. The secret is its amazing skin, which it changes to blend with its surroundings, startle prey, scare away predators, and signal to mates and rivals.

No one has decoded what all the different colors and shapes mean for all the different octopus species (though in many species, an octopus who turns red is excited, and one who is white is relaxed). But scientists do have a good idea how octopus skin works.

Small muscles in the skin can pull it into the peaks called papillae. For its color palette, the octopus uses three layers of three different types of cells near the skin's surface. The topmost cells are called chromatophores (cro-MAT-uh-fores). Each chromatophore cell is like a little pot of color enclosed in an elastic sac. When the octopus chooses to change color, it can use its muscles to open and to reveal a lot or a little of each pot—or not. It can make each chromatophore as big as seven times its resting (and invisible) diameter. The chromatophores may contain the colors yellow, red, brown, and black (depending on the species of octopus).

A middle layer of cells, the iridophores (eh-RID-uh-fores), can create an array of glittering blues, greens, and golds. By using iridophores in combination with chromatophores, for instance, the octopus can create colors such as purple and orange. The iridophore cells don't open and close, but the octopus can change the angle of each cell to reflect light like a tiny mirror.

At the deepest layer of skin are the octopus's leucophores (LEW-kuh-fores). These, too, reflect light, but instead of glittering colors they can create a white shine.

How does the octopus know which colors to turn? Scientists aren't sure. Especially because they have determined, by counting the different light-receiving pigments in the octopus eye, that octopuses are *colorblind!*

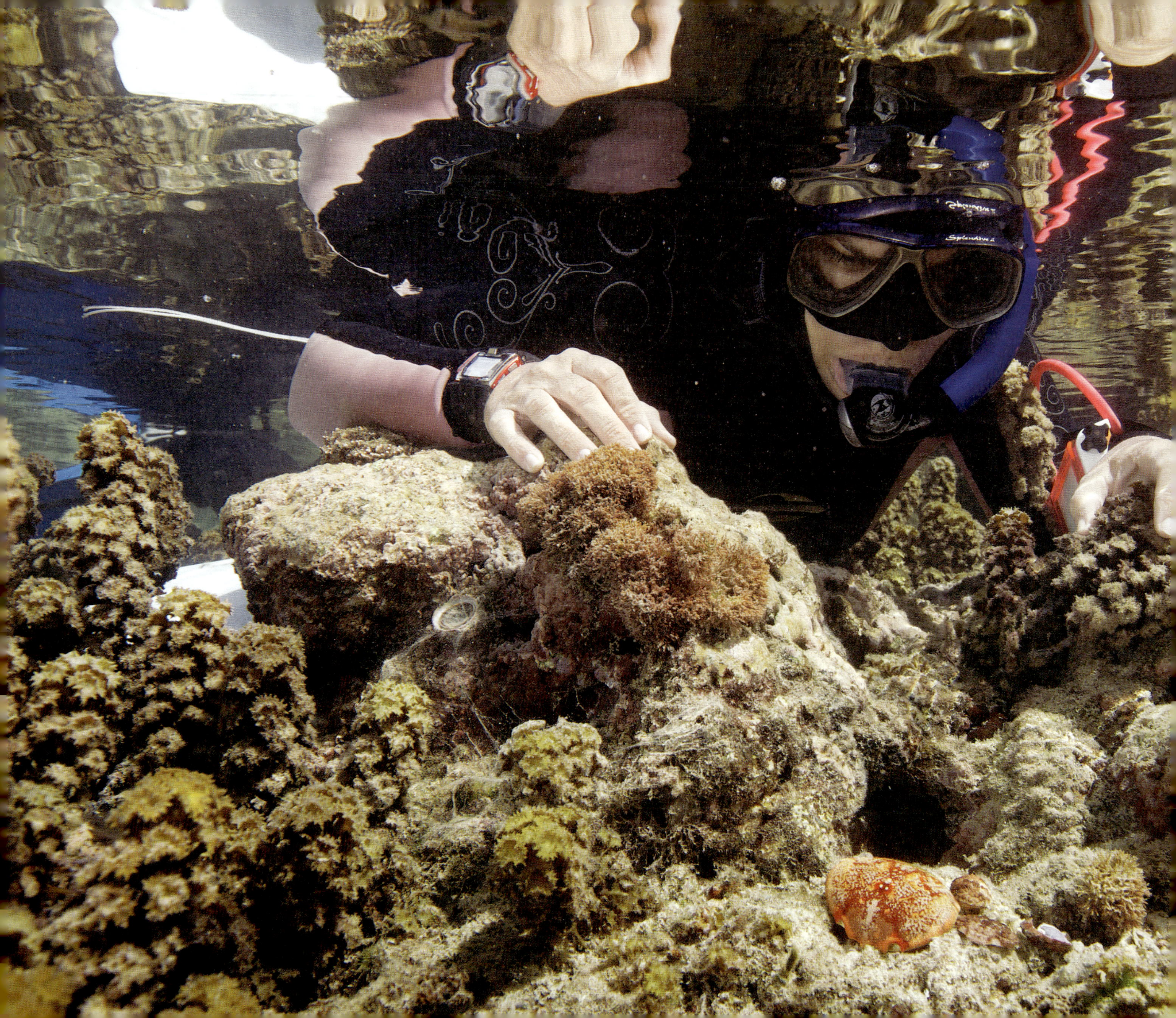

CHAPTER 6

We celebrate the start of the second week of our stay in Moorea by trying a new fruit.

So far we have sampled papaya, mango, pineapple, coconut . . . and now we prepare to open the light green soursop Jennifer bought at the side of the road. About the size of a Nerf football, covered with small, soft claw-shaped hooks, it looks like something that would grow on Mars. David and I peel it, revealing sweet-smelling white flesh studded with bean-size black seeds.

But it has an unfortunate consistency. Maybe the fruit is past its prime.

"Looks like snot," I observe. "Mixed with eyeballs."

"But in a good way," David adds optimistically. We taste it and it's not bad: delicately sweet, with a mild citrus flavor. But in our mouths, it feels like cotton coated in slime. No one else wants to eat it. "It looks like a dead octopus," Tatiana says—at which point we throw it away.

I don't dare say it, but I hope the fruit is not a bad omen. Today could be a crucial crossroads: the research can't proceed as planned without at least a second study site, and ideally, we'd like a third or fourth site as well. Time is running out.

Much like the soursop, things look good when we start out in our small caravan. We're eager to investigate the inviting new site Tatiana and David discovered. We pull over next to the dive shop and find ourselves among sweet little bungalows with thatched roofs set among flowering red hibiscus bushes and hot pink bougainvillea. We're instantly welcomed by the French-speaking groundskeeper, who tells us we can even use the hose onsite to rinse off when we emerge and can sit beneath a shady grove of coconut and banana trees to eat our picnic sandwiches.

The approach to the water is easy. A gentle slope of almost pure white sand (no hiding stonefish or sea cucumbers to step on!) makes for easy wading and leads to turquoise water deep enough to comfortably swim through. Free of the annoying algae, we see live corals, some as big as cars, and waving fields of light amber sea anemones. Named after flowers, anemones are not plants but predatory animals related to corals and jellyfish. They live in large groups, attaching themselves to the surface beneath them with sticky feet, harpooning small fish and shrimp with organs called nematocysts (neh-MAT-uh-cysts) and injecting their prey with stinging venom. White, orange, and black clownfish are immune to the venom. They shelter from predators among the sea anemones' stinging tentacles, looking as comfy as people sitting on a plush couch.

"It seems like paradise here," says Tatiana. "But is it paradise for octopuses?"

The place proves to be a paradise indeed. At first you notice only the showy fish, the ones with bold stripes and neon colors. But the more you look, the more you see: in the coral crevices, a pale, almost see-through catfish probes the sand with sensitive whiskers. But wait—there are two! No, three! No—six! And then the face of an electric blue chromis pops out from another crack in the coral . . .

"This is a really different habitat here," says Jennifer. "This could be important." If there are octopuses here, they might be eating different prey from those at Church Copse.

We are finding much larger fish than we found elsewhere. Jennifer signals to me as we swim together, pointing to one of the most stunning fish in the ocean: the Picasso triggerfish, which can grow to more than ten inches long. Against the canvas of a yellow and tan body, zany stripes of blue and black adorn the head; a brushstroke of electric yellow slashes the cheek. No wonder it's named for the cubist painter. Like all triggerfish, it can use spines on its back to lock itself immovably into coral crevices. When the tallest fin is up, it's locked into place with a shorter spine. To unlock, the fish depresses a third spine, known as the "trigger." Many people think fish are silent, but they're not. This fish grunts like a pig. No human is sure what it's saying. After seeing it, Jennifer and I both surface to gasp, "Wow!" (It's also the state fish of Hawaii, where in the local language it's called Humuhumunukunkuapua'a.)

But alas, no octopus. "It looks good here, but it ain't," Jennifer announces. "I'm getting absolutely nothing."

Nobody else is either. "If my bloodhounds can't find octopus here," she says, "there is no octopus. We need a new site."

So we swim ashore, remove our masks and fins, and strip off our wetsuits. Using fallen coconuts like stools, we eat our sandwiches in the shade of banana trees—then bid the idyllic site goodbye.

On Tatiana and David's weekend expedition, they had heard of another possibility: fishermen told them they often catch octopuses in an area just down the road. So off we go. We pull on our wetsuits, wade in, don our fins and masks.

And in fact, the site looks promising. There seem to be many good holes for octopuses. But we find no one at home. "Looks like the fishermen got here first," says Tatiana. We peel off our wetsuits again (protecting the car seats from the salt water and us from getting too hot) and drive on.

We stop next near a resort beside a channel with boat traffic and a small dock—the sort of place, notes Jennifer, that an octopus might find productive hunting grounds. We tug on our

Close-up of a toby pufferfish, one of the many colorful fish in the coral reef.

46

A rare encounter with a humphead wrasse.

The moray eel is a predator of the octopus.

wetsuits again and wade out to find a nice sandy bottom with a mix of coral rubble and living coral. David finds crab remains right away.

We try deeper water this time. "You get out like this on the edge of a reef," says David, "and you get the feeling you could see just anything!"

And indeed, we witness many splendors: A foot-long trumpet fish, long and slender, rests in the bowl of a coral. These lurk-and-lunge predators can change color, and often pretend to be just another piece of the coral where they hide. A boxfish with an orange head and blue and yellow spots uses its fluttering fins to hover as gently as a blimp.

Jennifer, David, Tatiana, and Keely all find sites that look like good dens for octopuses. But you never know whom you might find when you look into one of these holes. Keely comes face-to-face with a fat green moray eel, showing its needlelike teeth with every breath. These handsome marine eels, of which there are two hundred species, have a second set of pointy teeth in their throat, to make sure their struggling prey—such as an octopus—can't easily escape. Sometimes an octo loses an arm or two (which it can regrow) to a moray, and escapes with its life. Sometimes the octopus isn't so lucky.

Maybe that's what happened to the octopuses here. For there don't seem to be any now.

"We need to get out, look at some maps, and regroup," says Jennifer. Dejectedly we heave our once weightless bodies from the beautiful, clear water and head back to CRIOBE.

We gather in the collections room to discuss our options. We consult Google Earth. "Right on the edge of the boat channel and the bay and the reef—that's where we found octopuses before. And we should again," says Jennifer. She reminds us we are making progress.

"We have at least four octopuses. We have hundreds of data points around the dens. And we have a good idea how to find more."

"Besides," adds Tatiana, "it's important to know where the octopus is—but it's also important to know where they aren't. It's all part of the research. Every time we get in the water, we know a little bit more about what octopus habitat looks like. Every time we put our heads in the water, we're closer to finding what we need to know."

A giant manta ray swoops overhead.

RAINFORESTS OF THE OCEANS

Corals often look more like plants than animals. This is a close-up of a hard coral that belongs to a group called Fungia, which looks like a fungus.

A coral reef looks like a fantasy world from a 1960s psychedelic poster. Corals shaped like the lips of giants pout in Day-Glo purple. Sea fans more delicate than the finest lace seem to throb bright orange. The shapes of the creatures here look like brains or feathers, flames or antlers; they may come in crimson, gold, hot pink, or baby blue. They may remind you of the pillars of Greek temples or the plates on your dinner table; they're shaped like tiny volcanoes or the stalagmites in caves. But often, corals look like nothing you have ever seen before even in your wildest dreams—and they are all the more astonishing because they are *alive*.

Coral reefs are called the rainforests of the oceans because they are so complex, so rich in species, and so beautiful. But perhaps what is most amazing about corals is that they are not rocks or plants. A coral reef is an underwater world landscaped with animals—in partnership with plants living inside the animals' own cells.

A single coral animal is a small creature about the size of a pencil eraser and shaped like a little cup. Each coral has tiny, weakly stinging tentacles surrounding an opening that both takes in floating food and excretes wastes. But a coral doesn't just wait for its meal to arrive like a delivered pizza. Each also has a sort of vegetable garden—inside its own body! One-celled plants live in the coral animal's tissues. These algae, like all plants, capture sunlight to make food, and give much of their food to the coral. The different kinds of algae are what give the corals their spectacular colors.

You seldom see a coral animal by itself. They group together by the thousands and by the millions, creating great colonies of genetically identical siblings attached to the sea floor.

Coral animals are related to jellyfish. But unlike jellyfish, each coral animal has a skeleton, made out of limestone. Those species known as reef corals grow massive skeletons, which form the framework for tropical reefs—the richest ecosystems in the seas.

Coral reefs need very special conditions to grow. They thrive only in warm, clean, bright, shallow waters. Coral reefs comprise only .2 percent of the ocean surface—occupying only a tenth of the space the world's rainforests do. Yet between 10 and 15 percent of the seafood upon which people around the world depend comes from coral reefs. Turtles and fish come from deeper water to feed and breed among the reef's nooks and crevices. And reefs, importantly, protect land from erosion, softening the bite of the ocean's waves.

Even under ideal conditions, most species of coral grow less than an inch a year. And conditions these

Moorea's coral reefs are starting to recover. The yellow and black fish is a Moorish idol; its companion, a regal angelfish.

days are rarely ideal. Storms and earthquakes periodically destroy reefs; they are attacked by population explosions of coral-eating animals such as crown-of-thorns starfish; they are vulnerable to coral diseases and can get sick just like people do. And as the world grows more crowded with people and pollutants, coral diseases are on the rise.

People are making life far more hazardous for corals and all who depend on them. We crush them with our boats. We pierce them with anchors and drills. We poison them with oil spills and chemicals. We smother them with sewage and with runoff from the land. Possibly worst of all, carbon dioxide from burning coal, petroleum, and natural gas changes the chemistry of the ocean, crippling reefs. Many scientists worry that a great many corals may not survive. Already one-fifth of the world's coral reefs have been lost due to human interference; scientists estimate that more than a third of those that remain may die by 2050—unless people choose to reverse the damage.

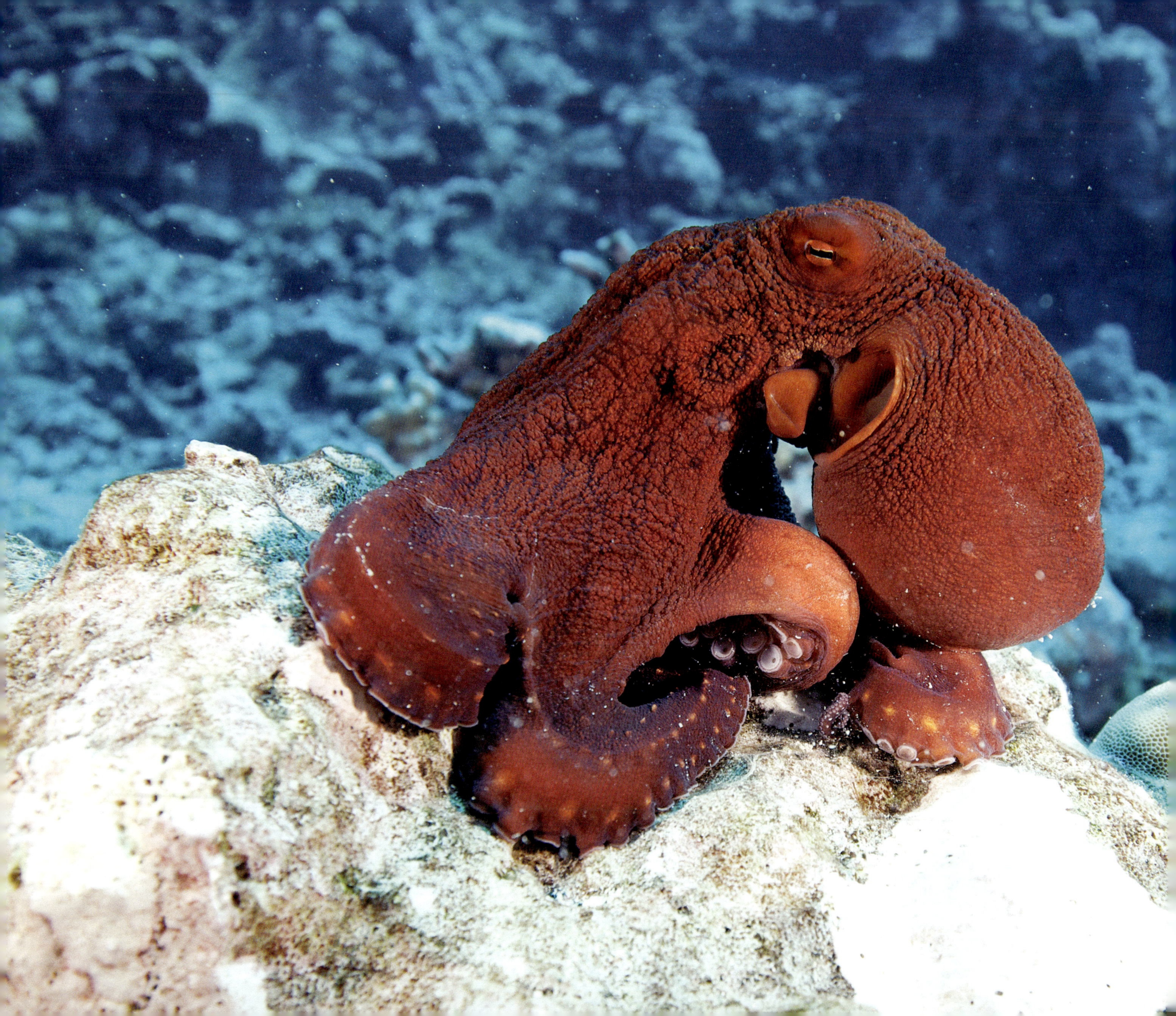

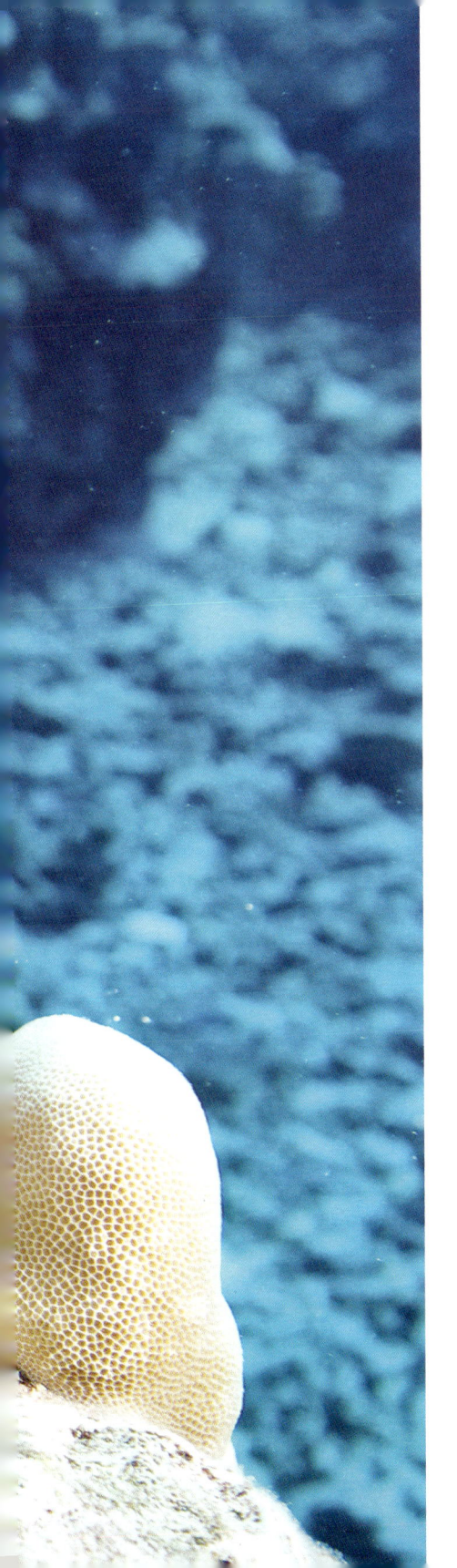

CHAPTER 7

By the next day, Tatiana and David have selected several new potential study sites along the bay on Google Maps. Jennifer and I set out with Tatiana in one of the pickup trucks to scout a site half an hour's drive south, nearly to the bottom of the heart shape that is Moorea. We're looking for a channel that brings nutrients to shallows carpeted with the sort of rubble where octopuses like to den.

On the way, we stop to investigate a lagoon—a shallow stretch of salt water separated from the sea by a sandbank or coral reef. The three of us wade out. But we don't even need to get in over our knees before we reach our conclusion: "It's another Sea Cucumber World," says Tatiana. "Let's go."

We drive on until we find a pullover near our site, just past a little village called Ha'apiti. "Looks very shallow," observes Jennifer. But Tatiana wants to take a look. We wade out. We don't even bother to bring our fins, it's so shallow. Within two minutes, still in water only calf-deep, Tatiana bends down and picks up a crab shell. "This is good octopus habitat," Tatiana announces. "This is going to be a good place—let's look." Two minutes later Tatiana turns toward us and beckons:

"Big octopus here!"

Jennifer and I hurry over. It's too shallow to swim, so we walk—trying not to stir up the muddy bottom or twist our ankles on the coral and rock beneath our feet.

The octopus is out hunting, probing the crevices in the rubble with the tips of its arms. It doesn't seem at all upset by the three humans looming over it. The animal is the biggest we've seen yet—the head and mantle are bigger than a grapefruit—and it shows us an astonishing combination of colors. Covered with papillae, the top exactly matches the yellow, green, and brown of the algae and seaweed here. But the arms are red with black spots! White eyes with black horizontal pupils swivel to look up at us.

"Oh, God, octopus—you're beautiful!" cries Tatiana. "Hi, beautiful guy!"

The octopus isn't far from its den. Just a foot away, we see a perfect little cave among the rubble—and just outside its entrance, the midden, littered with clam shells and the claws and carapace of a crab stretching five inches across.

"Let's do the personality test right now!" says Jennifer. Tatiana's and her slates are back at the car; this was just a scouting expedition, and nobody expected to find an octopus in four minutes! But I have my slate, and we remember the protocol. On our approach, the octopus does not retreat or change color, but looks up at us. When Tatiana touches the animal with the pencil, the octopus moves away slowly, reddens, spreads its arms, and continues exploring holes for prey.

The octopus withdraws its third right arm and Tatiana sees the tip clearly. Now she knows the sex: this is a female, because she has suckers all the way to the tip. A male would not, for his third right arm has a specialized tip called the ligula (LIG-you-la) that he uses to place a sperm packet inside the female's mantle opening, like tucking a gift into a pocketbook. When Jennifer collects the shells around the burrow, the female continues foraging, but always keeps an eye on the scientist. Perhaps the octopus assumes the human is hunting for prey too!

It takes Jennifer more than a minute to collect all the shells from around the site, more than fit in her collection bucket. We stuff the overflow, including a sand crab carapace six inches across, into a Ziploc bag. (Later, we discover we still didn't get it all: when Keith and I return to the site that afternoon, we find another huge carapace of a sand crab within six feet of the den. Or maybe the octopus had just consumed another snack in the interim.)

"Looks like she's been in this den for a long period," says Tatiana. Because octopuses usually move to new dens every few days, the hunting must be exceptionally good in this area. The octopus is beautiful, healthy, and strong—like Tatiana's mother. So Tatiana names the animal after her: Cassia. Tatiana takes a photo with her underwater camera for our records, and to email to her mom.

"This octopus is wonderfully bold!" exclaims Jennifer. As we mark the den with a buoy, Cassia uses her funnel to blow a small volcano of sand toward us. Not wanting to harass her, we leave her behind and explore the rest of the area.

Jennifer is impressed. "Look at all these wonderful caves! This is a perfect habitat! There are lots of crabs, there are probably clams in the sand, and so many perfect hiding places."

As a graduate student, Jennifer had explored, in the lab, how octopuses pick their homes. "What impressed me most was the octopuses seemed to have an image in their mind of the best home—as we do," she said. "I'd like to have a home with a sheltered porch, or a spare bedroom, or near a good school. But unlike in a laboratory, in the real world of the sea, the octopus has to take the best it can get, and then fix it up."

This may be what Cassia was just doing. Octopuses frequently excavate sand by using their

An octopus probes crevices with the tips of its arms.

A hawksbill sea turtle.

funnels like leaf blowers. They also bring rocks and shells to the front of their dens for added security, sometimes carrying them for quite a distance. (In response to a predator near the den, an octopus may hold up a shell or rock in front of it like a shield.) And some octopuses even clip the algae in front of their homes, the way a homeowner would trim a hedge.

We wade on, and Jennifer starts finding dens everywhere. "Now, here's one for sure," she says, pointing out a little grotto. "Just because it's not occupied now doesn't mean it wasn't occupied last week—or that it won't be next week, or even tomorrow!"

Meanwhile, at the opposite end of the island, past Cook's Bay, Keely and David are checking out another site that looked promising on Google Earth. They find white sand flecked with living corals, shallows alive with colorful fish, easy swimming, and comfortable wading—the sort of place, Keely later tells me, where honeymooners would love to snorkel.

"But we don't want that," she says. "Honeymooners' paradise is not for octopus!" No, we need to be scraping our chests on sharp edges of dead coral and getting hit in the face with stocky, thorny, pinecone-y algae while struggling to swim in two feet of water.

So David and Keely leave paradise. Determined to find octopuses, they head back to a spot near Bent Palm, just east of our first study site, Church Copse.

Sure enough, the shallows there are full of sharp coral skeletons and annoying algae. Keely and David split up. Bumping their knees and scraping their fingers on coral skeletons, both are finding crab and clam shells. Keely starts following what she thinks might be a foraging trail—a succession of trash a hunting octopus left, snacking as it traveled and leaving the shells behind. But octopuses prefer to consume their takeout meals in the safety of their homes, and Keely hopes the trail will lead to an octopus in its den.

After fifteen minutes of looking, David signals to Keely that it's time to go back. A team of French students will be waiting for the other truck to return. Darn! Keely just glimpsed a hawksbill turtle swimming near the edge of the channel, and hates to leave. Reluctantly, she turns to swim toward shore, keeping her eyes on the rocky bottom as she snorkels, just in case.

Rock, dead coral, algae, another rock. And then: shells. Lying by a rock—with another rock lying in front of it at an odd angle. "I thought, 'That rock wouldn't just be sitting there,'" Keely tells me later. "Somebody must have *put* it there." She dives to investigate, and, sure enough, the rock partially blocks a hole. And in the hole . . .

"OCTOPUS!" she calls to David. He swims over. They high-five. And since Tatiana named her octopus after her mother, so does Keely. And the name really fits, especially since with her discovery, we have not only a second study site, but a third: Joy!

OCTOPUS INFLUENCE

With their superhuman strength, seemingly magical skin, and eerie intelligence, octopuses have inspired artists, storytellers, and even religious leaders from coastal cultures around the world. In the Gilbert Islands of the Pacific, an octopus god, Na Kika, was said to be the son of the first beings. It's lucky for us land-dwellers that he was born, the story goes: with his many strong arms, Na Kika shoved up the earth from the bottom of the sea to create the islands. The coastal tribes of British Columbia and Alaska revere the octopus as a medicine animal. Tradition holds that the octopus wields power over the weather and is able to restore health to the sick. Hawaiian myths tell how our current world is really the remnant of a previous one, and the only survivor of that prehistory is the octopus. Ancient Peruvians also held the octopus in high esteem, though it's not known which of its many powers were revered. We know they appreciated them because of the beautiful gold sculptures of octopuses that the people left behind.

To Moorea's seafaring people, the strong, many-armed octopus was considered the island's divine protector, its reaching arms a symbol of peace and unity. In fact, today the symbol of the environmental management plan for the many groups working together to protect Moorea's sea creatures, Plan de Gestion de l'Espace Maritime (Marine Space Management Plan), is an octopus. Its eight arms point to the eight most critical areas designated for special protection.

Across from the community center, near the "octopus church" a mural depicts a tattooed fisherman.

In the village that is now called Papetoai, just a short drive from CRIOBE, there was once a temple dedicated to the octopus. Today, a Protestant church occupies that site. Built in 1827, it's the oldest church in Moorea. When Keith and I visited it for Sunday services, the pastor, wearing a long garland of colorful flowers, took us outside to show us the view of Mount Rotui; he told us it looks like the profile of an octopus. And today, it's easy to see that the pretty church, which faces the sea, still celebrates the octopus: it has eight sides!

A young member of the congregation of the "octopus church" shown at right.

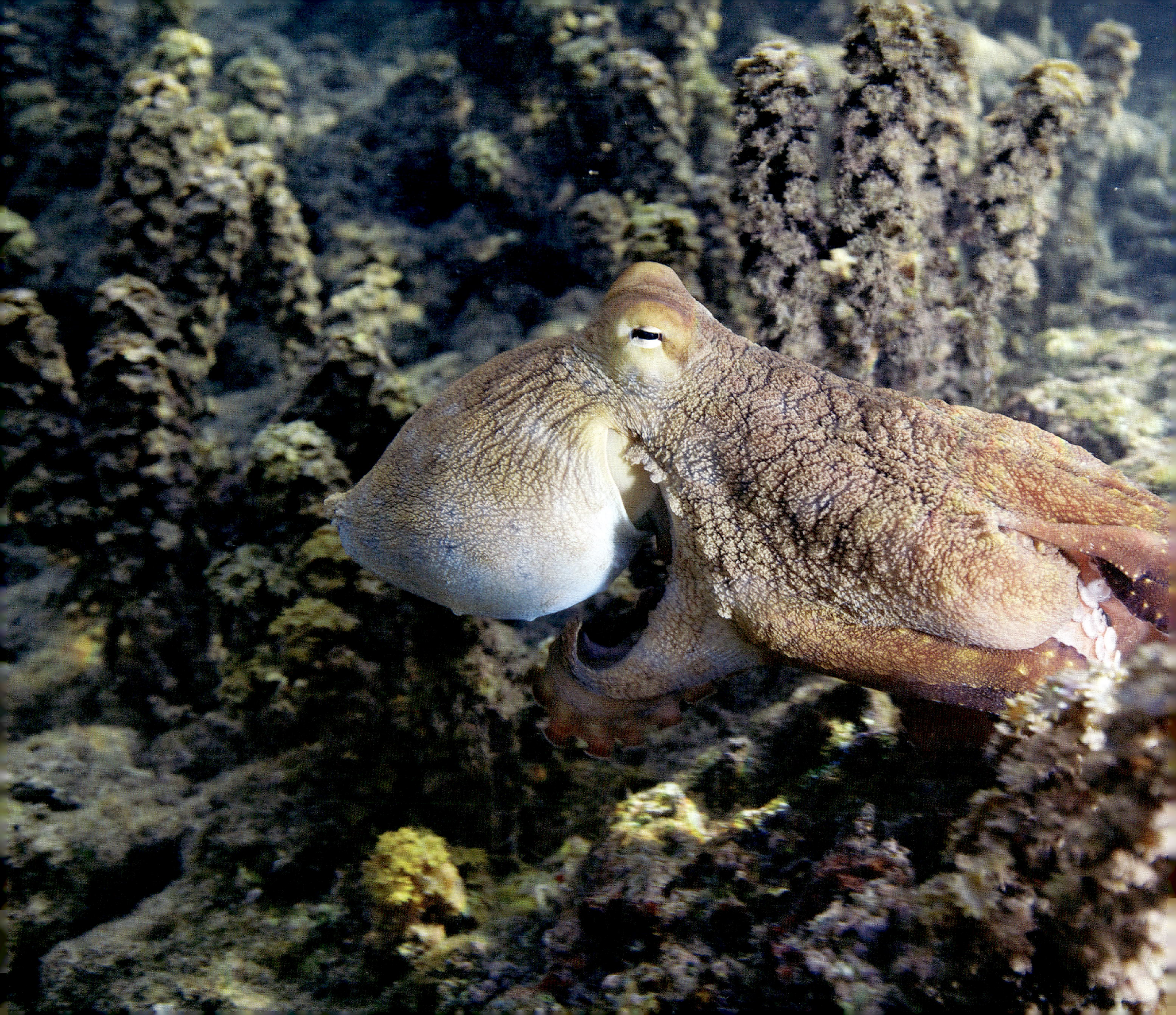

CHAPTER 8

The next morning, we head to Bent Palm. Keely is eager to give Joy the personality test. And we're all eager to find out whether Joy has neighbors.

Keely beelines to Joy's buoy, dive slate in hand. Jennifer and I wait a few feet back so as not to interfere. Keely dives, stays under, and surfaces. She's done the first part of the personality test, recording the octopus's behavior upon approach.

"What's Joy like?" asks Jennifer.

"Already, this octopus is like my mother!" reports Keely. Next to two ivory-colored clam shells resting eight inches from the den opening, lying bowl-side up below the hole, the octopus was asleep in its little grotto. Joy did not seem to appreciate being awoken. She retreated farther into her den, like a sleepy person burrowing deeper into the covers. "When my mom's asleep, she's like, 'Leave me be!'" Keely tells us.

Now for the "touch" portion of the test. Keely dives again. A minute later, she surfaces to report: "Mmmnmph!" Pulling out her snorkel, she tells us the reason for her excitement: "Joy held my pencil pretty good. A tug of war over a pencil—perfect for a mother-daughter relationship!"

Now she hands her dive slate to Jennifer so she can collect the prey remains. The den is in the shallows, just a foot and a half deep. A crab carapace is wedged into a hole. Unlike Joy, Keely is constrained by elbows and wrists and can't reach it. She needs both hands.

Keely fills the collection bucket with remains as Jennifer rejoices. "That Joy has a healthy appetite!" The octopus seems annoyed. She holds her arms over her head, white suckers facing outward in a position Jennifer calls "crown of suckers," and she is bright red—a color often shown by an octopus who is irritated or excited.

It is probably a relief for Joy to see us finning away from her at last. David is waving to us from two hundred yards away. Has he found another den? We swim toward him slowly, our faces in the water. At first I can't see what he's pointing at. All I see is a lumpy rock about nine inches tall and a foot wide, covered with reddish algae. But then, like those Magic Eye drawings, the image springs suddenly clear: It's an octopus, coiled on its arms atop its den, the baggy body hanging down in front like a fat nose, its hyphen-slit eyes on top of the head clearly watching us. The animal is fully alert, covered with papillae and red with excitement—except for a white blaze down

and white, its papillae forming jagged peaks all over its body, each bump standing up much taller than it is wide. The mottling looks like feathers; the pointy papillae over the eyes look like ear tufts. If we weren't underwater, we might think we were face-to-face with a small owl.

But its resemblance to an owl stops the moment it lifts off its rock and begins to move.

An octopus in motion looks like nothing else—or like everything else but an octopus. Sometimes it's a silken scarf floating in the water. Other times it's a snail, gliding on its suckers along the bottom as smoothly as a boat on the sea. Sometimes it's a jet, propelling off faster than you can swim, shooting water out its funnel as its arms trail behind. Sometimes it's a beating heart, throbbing with each breath of water entering its gills. And sometimes it's the sea itself, pouring through a hole like water down a drain.

Which is just what this new, small octopus does before our astonished eyes.

I pull my head out of the water and call to David. "The octopus was on the move!" I yell.

"Mine is too!" he answers.

Now we gather again around David's octopus and watch in fascination as it crawls along the bottom. Each moment is a revelation. As the octopus turns to its left, it reveals the full length of its arms—and I gasp through my snorkel. The front three arms all end halfway down—surely the result of an encounter with a predator. In an instant, we get a glimpse of a dramatic, defining moment in this octopus's personal history.

the center of the face and body that reminds me of my border collie at home.

While we gather around just a foot away, the animal stays atop the rock as if posing for photos. Finally it moves. One of the right arms emerges from beneath it and then slides inside the octopus's gill opening—the octopus equivalent of scratching an itch in your nose.

We are so mesmerized by the creature that no one has noticed that Keely has left. Then from beneath the water, even with muffled ears, we hear her call: "I have another one! And it's hunting!"

David stays with his octopus and I swim over to see Keely's. But where is it? Again, despite Keely pointing directly at the animal, it's absurdly difficult to find—even with the image of a camouflaged octopus fresh in my mind.

That's because this octopus doesn't look at all like David's. This one's much smaller, perhaps only six inches tall. And it's a totally different color and shape. It's a uniformly mottled brown

63

The skin is healing over, but the arms have not yet started to regrow. It is impossible not to feel a pang of sympathy. We imagine its dramatic struggle to escape. Was it exploring a hole when it encountered a moray eel? Was it attacked by a shark? Did it fight off the predator with its strong remaining arms? Or did it squirt out ink and jet away?

Surely the octopus remembers its brush with death. Jennifer's studies, as well as others', show that octopuses can recall events for months, even years. But the scary memory hasn't dampened this animal's zest for discovery. It keeps us large, potentially dangerous mammals in view, but doesn't try to hide from us. Instead, it begins crawling along the bottom, revealing more of itself as it moves.

Curious, the octopus reaches toward me with its intact second right arm. It tastes the neoprene of my glove with several of its white suckers, then gently withdraws. Now we can see the third right arm too. Suckers run all the way to the tip. This is a female—a second piece of precious biographical information about this distinctive individual, who seems to be happy to show us a piece of her world.

She clearly keeps an eye on us as she moves over the ocean bottom, but she does not seem afraid. Abruptly she changes color. Three long rows of light spots spring to her legs, while the background color changes from red to a dark brown. Her head and body assume a mottled brown. Then she suddenly flashes white!

What do these color changes mean? They certainly don't all blend in with her surroundings. But camouflage, as Jennifer later explained, doesn't always mean looking exactly like your background. "All that's really important is that you don't look like an octopus," she said. Certain colors, patterns, and shapes make an octopus look like something bigger and more dangerous than it really is. Sometimes an abrupt change in color or pattern is enough to startle a predator away. And it's important to remember that the show isn't always meant for human eyes: the octo's audience might be a bird looking down from the air above, or a shark off to one side—or even another octopus. All of these creatures have very different kinds of eyes. Some, like birds, see in brilliant color—others, like turtles, do not. Lighting is different from above than below. And things look different to a bird or mammal in air than to a fish in water.

Now the octopus smooths her skin, turns a fawn color, and jets off like a squid.

We follow. In a few yards, she alights, turns a darker brown, re-erects her papillae, and resumes her travels on her arms. If she were a person, she'd be awkwardly walking on her knees and elbows, but since she has no bones, her gait seems more graceful glide than stride.

It's hard to tell how long we spent following this large, bold octopus. Time feels different underwater. We felt as if we had entered a different world. We were on octopus time, and they don't wear waterproof wristwatches. It seemed like a dream: in our regular lives above water, nothing like what we witnessed would be possible—yet here it was happening. We were caught like dreamers in the drama unfolding before us.

At one point, the octopus grew a new pair of "eyes." A set of two-and-a-half-inch blue rings appeared suddenly, one on each side of her body. These are known as ocelli (oh-SELL-ee), a word that comes from the Latin word for "eye." They look like eyes, but they're not. They're convincing enough to fool a predator, though. It's easy to imagine how big eyes like these might belong to a much bigger animal. Or maybe they signal, "Your sneak attack is foiled: I see you!"

At another point, the octopus was poised atop some coral rubble with many holes, into which she inserted at least four, probably more, of her arms. The whole time, she looked directly at us, the skin around her eyes making a starburst pattern of white rays. But her look was far away, like that of a person fishing in both pockets for some keys.

The octopus didn't find anything to eat while we were with her. Maybe we were wrecking her hunt. Though we were having a blast, David eventually pulled his head from the water and suggested we should go. We didn't want to harass her—especially since she had been such a splendid hostess.

David named his octopus Mary Lou, after his mother. Keely named hers Zeus, after her cat. Meeting them, just two days before I had to leave Moorea, was a turning point in the expedition. All of a sudden, it seemed octopuses were almost everywhere.

"All we needed to do was get our eyes," said Tatiana. "It's almost magic," agreed David. "You don't know why you want to turn over that rock, but you begin to develop an intuition." For Keely, it seemed she had better luck when she was not specifically looking: "The times I've found them," she said, "I'm bombing over someplace else—and then I find the perfect midden, look in front of it, and there's an octopus! The other times, it's almost like I'm trying too hard."

But Jennifer, the most experienced of us all, had confidence all along. "I told you I had bloodhounds—and we found octopuses!" she said.

The next day, we returned to Ha'apiti to look for more octopuses but found only Cassia—the lonely queen of her deserted octopus kingdom. (Keith found a large moray living there, and we wondered whether it had eaten the neighbors.) But the following day, back at Bent Palm, we visited Joy, who was holding her arms in the shape of a handlebar mustache in her den. As Jennifer pointed her out to me, Tatiana found a smaller octopus—was it Zeus?—out hunting between Mary Lou's and Joy's dens. The animal flowed into a hole, turning dark brown except for one arm, which was white. Not long after that, Keely called out that she had found another octopus, whom she named Frederick, after her dad.

And minutes later, Jennifer called to us. "Want another octopus?" At first contact, the animal turned dark, then pale. Jennifer named this one Charlotte, after her ten-year-old granddaughter. And Keely then discovered Christopher, named after her husband—the biggest octopus we had yet seen. "This is amazing!" said Tatiana. "It's almost ridiculous!" agreed Keely.

Our octo-luck even extended to other CRIOBE researchers. Students were seeing octopuses too—and one of the staff members even found a tiny baby octopus inside one of their tools, an oceanographic data logger, and brought it back to the wet lab. We observed it in an aquarium overnight before setting it free.

After Keith and I left, Tatiana, David, and Keely went scuba diving, but in a different place from where Keith and I had gone earlier. And there, on a barrier reef, forty-five feet deep, they discovered, photographed, and tested yet another octopus—and collected thirteen prey items from the midden around its den.

Next the team tried another, shallower research site. The University of California runs a field station, Gump Station, not far from CRIOBE on the former estate of the artist, composer, and businessman Richard B. Gump. The first day they went, it was windy and rough. The next day, the team showed up at nine a.m.—and by noon had found five more octopuses!

By now, the team had found so many octopuses that they had borrowed names from dogs, cats, spouses, and other relatives. But Jennifer had a good French name for the last animal of the day—and as it turned out, the last animal of the expedition: Finis!

P.S.

In all, the team found eighteen octopuses at five different sites; collected, sorted, and identified 244 shells and carapaces from octopus habitat; found the remains of 106 food items outside active octopus dens; and identified outside the occupied dens 41 different species of prey.

Interestingly, sites where octopuses had more varied menus also supported higher densities of octopuses—sort of the way cities, with lots of different restaurants, have more people packed into them than the suburbs, with fewer dining choices.

The team collected personality data on all eighteen octopuses—but four of them had too few leftover bits of shell by their dens to offer conclusions about their food preferences. Of the other fourteen, there was a small correlation between personality type and food preference: bolder octopuses were slightly more likely to sample more different kinds of food than shyer ones. "I regard this as interesting but not by any means conclusive," Jennifer said.

Did we solve all the questions we set out to answer? No—because of a problem nobody foresaw—which led to a discovery nobody expected. In Moorea, the same species of octopus acted differently than the octopuses previously studied in Hawaii! Unlike the *Octopus cyanea* previously studied, those in Moorea didn't stay long in their dens and didn't bring lots of prey home. Maybe they ate mostly "on the road."

Why the difference? Is it because Moorea has different octopus food than Hawaii? (Hawaii has more crabs.) Or could it be that Moorea octopuses aren't really *Octopus cyanea*? Could it be we were working with a new, unknown species of octopus? Or could the difference be due to the different habitats, or the variety of available foods, or the damage to Moorea's reefs—or something else?

As is often the case in science, our field expedition generated more questions than answers. "Science doesn't usually give you clear answers of the type you wanted, especially fieldwork," Jennifer said. "But we got information—that's what it's about!"

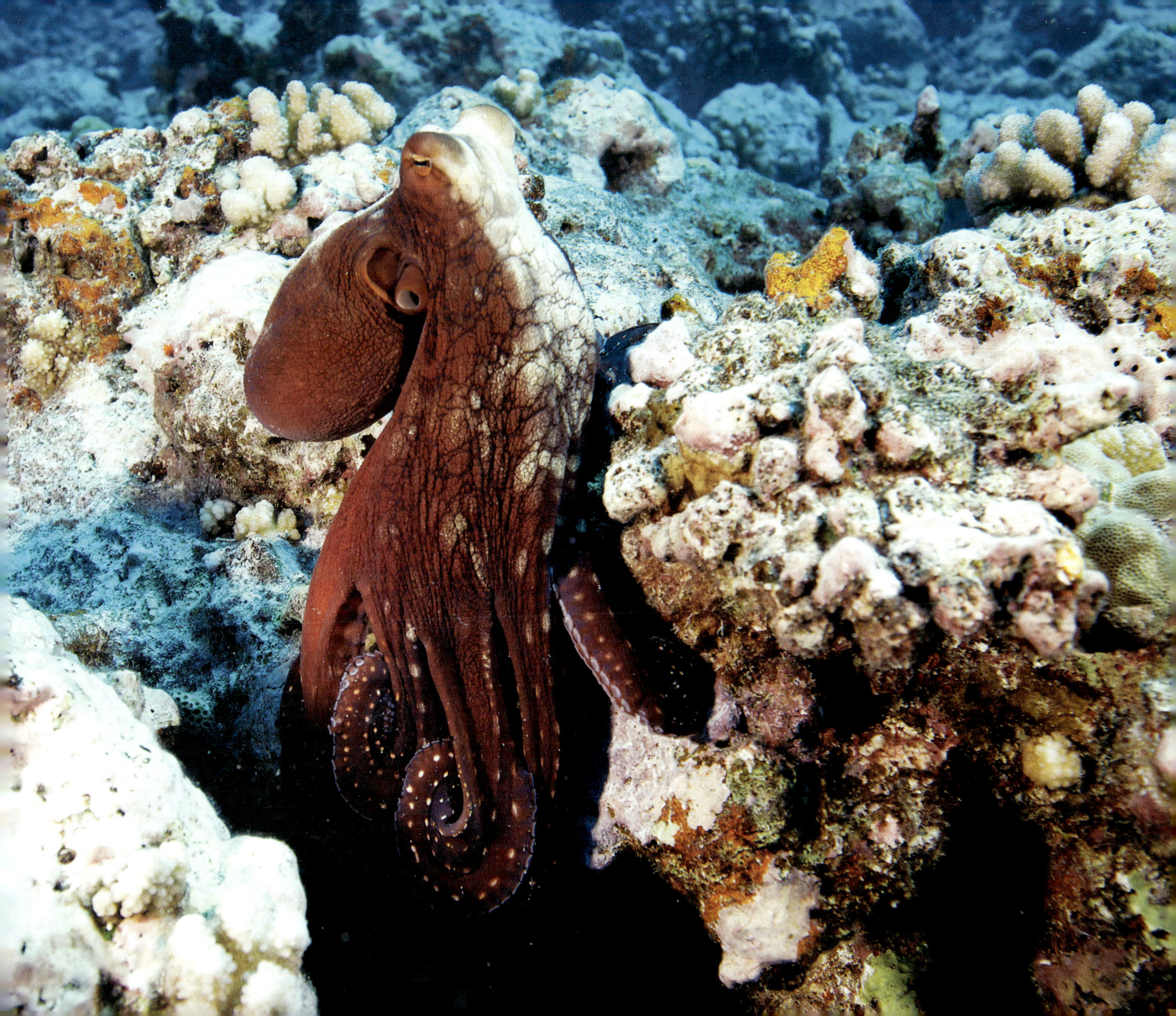

SELECTED BIBLIOGRAPHY

Cosgrove, James A., and Neil McDaniel. *Super Suckers: The Giant Pacific Octopus and Other Cephalopods of the Pacific Coast*. Madeira Park, B.C.: Harbour Press, 2009.

Cousteau, Jacques, and Philippe Diole. *Octopus and Squid: The Soft Intelligence*. New York: Doubleday, 1973.

Dunlop, Colin, and Nancy King. *Cephalopods: Octopus and Cuttlefishes for the Home Aquarium*. Neptune City, N.J.: T.F.H. Publications, 2009.

Lane, Frank. *Kingdom of the Octopus*. New York: Pyramid Publications, 1962.

Mather, Jennifer, Roland C. Anderson, and James B. Wood. *Octopus: The Ocean's Intelligent Invertebrate*. Portland, Ore.: Timber Press, 2010.

Williams, Wendy. *Kraken: The Curious, Exciting, and Slightly Disturbing Science of Squid*. New York: Abrams Image, 2011.

ACKNOWLEDGMENTS

In researching and photographing this book, we were honored to work with the wonderful people you have met in these pages. We thank them all. Many others, though, helped us from behind the scenes, and we'd like to thank them here. We could never have created this book without all the staff and students we met at CRIOBE, who generously shared their expertise, equipment, and experience with us. Back in the United States, we'd like to thank our superb editor, Kate O'Sullivan, and our book designer extraordinare, Cara Llewellyn. We are grateful to our many close friends at the New England Aquarium; to the late Roland Anderson at the Seattle Aquarium; to Paul Erikson; to Robert and Judith Oksner; to Jody Simpson; and to Howard Mansfield.

Though the ink on these pages isn't the kind they appreciate, we would also like to thank the octopuses we met in Moorea. We hope that you, our readers, will show *your* appreciation for octopuses everywhere by keeping their habitat—the oceans of the world—clean and wild and safe.

INDEX

Page numbers in **bold** refer to photos and illustrations.

algae, 28, **29**, 40, 50, 57
Anderson, Roland, 7, 25
arms, **11**
    ability to regrow, 11, 49, 64
    neurons in the, 11, 25
    tip, gender identification by, 54, 64
    tip, hunting in crevices with, 53, **55**, 65
    webbing between, **33**

beak, 1, 5, 9
Bent Palm, **vi**, 13, 57, 61, 65
birds, 5, 25, 65
blood, blue, 11
brain, 11, 25

camouflage, **iv–v**. See also color
    changing shape, 2, 16, 25, 41, 62
    sprouting papillae, 2, 43, 61, 62, 65
cephalopods, 11
Chancerelle family, 13, 39, **40**
church, **58**, 58–59, **59**
Church Copse, **vi**, 13, 14, 16, 21, 39
clams, 2, 5, 11, 16, **16**
classification, scientific, 11, 36–37
color, **42–43**
    ability to change, 2, 27, 41, 54
    and emotion, 32, 43, 61
    mechanism of change, 42–43
    observation of change, 9, 24, 32, 38, 64
conservation, 58
Cook's Bay, **vi**, 18, 57
coral, 50, **50**
coral reefs, 24, **44–45**
    as an ecosystem, 45–46, 50–51
    atoll, 13
    barrier, **vi**, 13, 66
    fringing, 13
    threats to, 18, 50–51

crabs, **3**, 5, 8, 23, 40, 54
CRIOBE research facility, 13, 18, **18–19**, 35, **36**
    location, **vi**
    researchers, **19**, 66
    specimen collection, **34–35**, 35–38, **37**

data collection, **26–27**, 27, 66
defense mechanisms, octopus, 2, 25, **28**, 65. See also camouflage; intelligence
dens, 17, 23, 25, 54, 57
diet, 66
    birds, 5
    crabs, **3**, 5, 8, 23, 40, 54
    mollusks, 5, 21, 40, 53, 57, 61
    other octopuses, 5, 8
    otter, 5
dolphins, **17**, 39

eel, moray, **48**, 48–49, 65
eggs, 10, 11, 32
Ellenbogen, Keith
    in the field, 31, 38–39, 65
    at the "octopus church," 59
    as photographer, 6, 28, 38–39, 41
emotion, 32, 43, 61
evolution, 2
extraterrestrials, 5
eyes, **11**, 43, 53, 61

field research, **26–27**
    challenges/joys, 17, 21, 28, 31, 57
    sites, **iv**, 13, 40, 45. See also specific sites
    use of Google Earth/Maps, 49, 53, 57
    vehicles, 13, 40, 41
fins, 11
fish
    angelfish, **51**
    ature, 16
    boxfish, 48
    butterfly fish, 15, 21
    catfish, 46
    clownfish, 45–46
    coral grouper, **25**
    hawkfish, 21
    hogfish, 16
    Moorish idol, **20–21**, 21, **51**

    Picasso triggerfish, 46
    pufferfish, 18, **46**
    spotted toby, 16
    stonefish, 28, 41
    trumpet fish, 48
    wrasse, 16, **47**
funnel, 1, 25, 54, 57, 62

gender identification, 54, 64
gills, 8, 11, 62
global warming, 6, 18, 51
Gump Station, **vi**, 66

Ha'apiti, **vi**, 53, 65
habitat, marine
    coral reef ecosystem, 45–46, 50–51
    humans in the, 28, 31, 57, 65
    northern coldwater, 8, 23
    percent of the planet, 1
    sandy bottom ecosystem, 14
    tropical Moorea, 1, 14–16, 21–22, 45–46, **51**, 54
head, 1, 5, 11, 32
hearts, 11
hemocyanin, 11
humans
    fishing/collection of octopus, 5–6, 46, **58**
    octopus influence on, **58**, 58–59, **59**
    in the underwater habitat, 28, 31, 65
hunting, 5, 53, **55**, 65

ink screen or ink blob, 2, **28**
intelligence, 25
    evolution of, 2
    fixing up a den, 54, 57
    identifying specific humans, 7, 25, 32
    imagination, 54
    memory, 64
    opening containers, 25
    watching to learn, 39, **39**
invertebrates, 2, 7
iridophores, 43

Langford, Keely, **9**, **36**
    background, 9–10, 27
    in the field, 40–41, 48, 57, 61–62, 65–66
    interpretive specialist, 6, 9

Leite, Tatiana, **9**
    background, 9
    love of the water, 9, 31
    in Sea Cucumber World, 14, 53
    skill in finding octopuses, 17, 24, **30**, 53, 65
    specialty in octopus species, 5, 9
    transect work, **8**, 39, 41
leucophores, 43
life span, 11, 32
ligula, 54

mantle, 11, **11**, 53, 54
Mather, Jennifer, **7**, **40**
    background, 2, 5, 7, 54
    field research plan, 5, 13
    specialty in psychology, 4, 5, 7, 25, 54, 64
    team built by, 4, 5, 6, 17
    using CRIOBE collection, 35–38
Menashi, Wilson, 25, 32
middens, 5, 17, 21, 23, 41, 53
mollusks, 2, 11
Montgomery, Sy, 6
    experience underwater, 65
    making friends with an octopus, 32
    at the "octopus church," 59
Moorea, **vi**, 1, 18, 45, **51**, 57
mouth, 11
movement, 1, **2**, 8, 62, 65
Murphy, Bill, 32
myths, octopus-based, 58

natural disasters, 18, 51
neurons, 11, 25
New England Aquarium, 25, 32

ocelli, 65
octopuses
    classification, 11
    common (*Octopus vulgaris*), 2, 5, 9, 25
    giant Pacific, 5, 7, 8, 10, 11, 25, 32
    glow-in-the-dark, 11
    influence on humans, **58**, 58–59, **59**
    making friends with, 32
    mimic, 5–6
    number of species, 1, 11
    Octopus wolfi, 11

Pacific day (*Octopus cyanea*), 2, 66
    pygmy, 2, 7
    red, 23
    tally for expedition, 66
    techniques to find, 17, 24, 65
    transparent, 11
octopuses, individual
    Athena, 32
    Cassia, 54, 65
    C.C., 10
    Charlotte, 66
    Christopher, 66
    Cleo, 24, 28, 35, 36, 39
    Clove, 10
    Emily Dickinson, 7
    Finis, 66
    Frederick, 65
    Godzilla!, 8
    Grover, 24, 28, 39
    Gwenevere, 25
    Joy, 57, 61, 65
    Jude, 8
    Kwila, 24, 28, 36
    Leisure Suit Larry, 7
    Mary Lou, 65
    Octavia, 32
    Zeus, 65
Opunohu Bay, **vi**, 18

Papetoai, 59, **59**
personality, 5, 7, 32, 39, 54, 61
pollution, 6, 8, 51
predators, 62, 64, 65
    humans, 5–6, 46
    moray eels, **48**, 48–49
    sharks, 2, 65

radula, 5
rays, **22**, 49
reproduction, 4, 5, 10, 54

Scheel, David, **8**
    background, 5, 8, 17
    data checklist by, 27
    specialty in behavioral ecology, 5, 8
    telemetry work, 8

    transect work, 40, 41
    using CRIOBE collection, 35–38, **37**
science
    generates more questions, 66
    teaching children, 9, 10
    women in, 7
sea cucumber, 14, **14**, 53
Seattle Aquarium, 2, 7, 25
sea urchin, 16, 28
shape, changing, 2, 16, 25, 41, 62
sharks, 2, **15**, 15–16, 39, 65
shells
    CRIOBE collection, **34–35**, 35–38, **37**
    as door to den, 25, 57
    as home for other creatures, 15
    octopus strategies to open, 5
    tally for expedition, 66
skin
    ability to taste with, 11
    cells which create color palette, 43
    ocelli, 65
    papillae, 2, 43, 61, 62, 65
starfish, 2, 18, 51
stomach, 11
suckers, 4, **11**
    ability to taste with, 11, 32, 64
    dexterity, 11, 17, 27, 61
    suction to open shells, 5

tags for radio telemetry, 8
teeth. *See* radula
threats to octopuses, 6, 8, 18. *See also* predators
tongue, 5
transect, habitat, **8**, 27, 39, 40–41
turtles, 18, 22, **23**, 50, **56–57**, 57, 65

Vancouver Aquarium, 6, 9, 10, 27
venom, 1, 5
vision, 43

weight, 2, 8

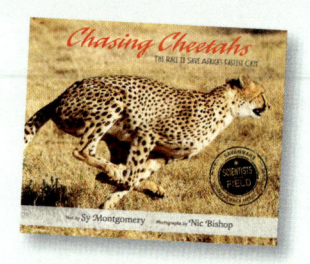

SCIENTISTS IN THE FIELD

Where Science Meets Adventure

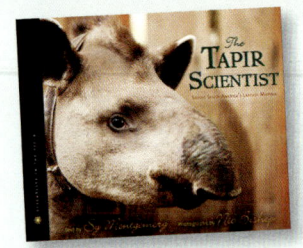

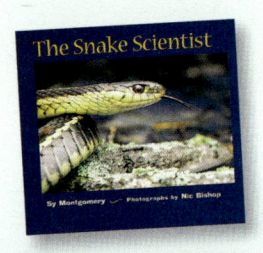

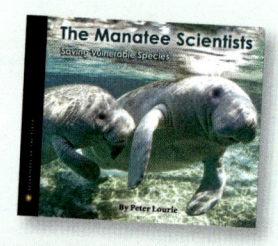

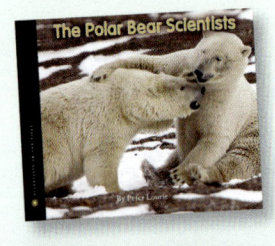

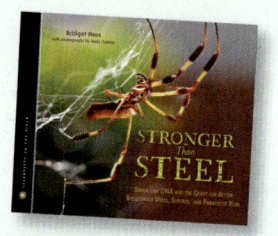

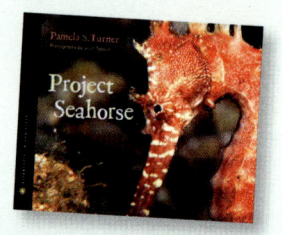

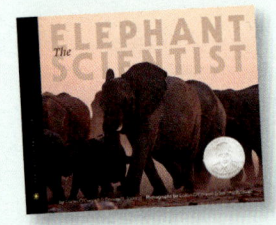

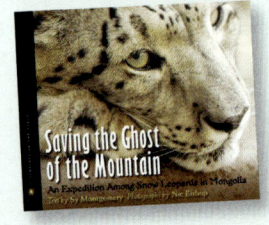

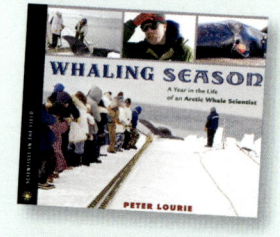

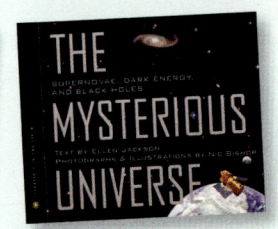

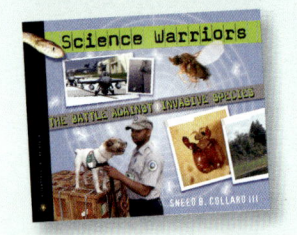

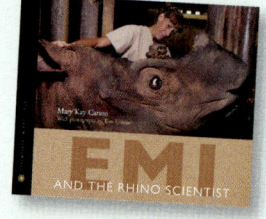

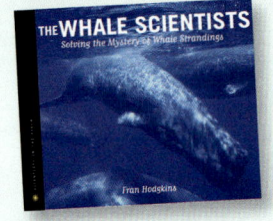

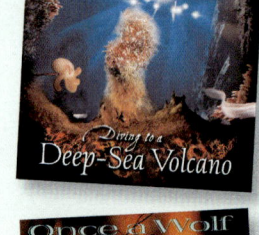

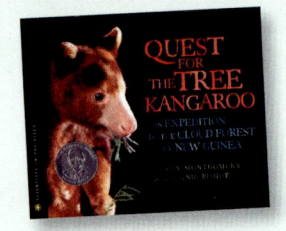

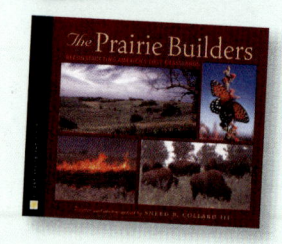

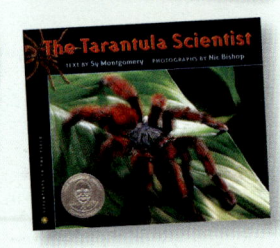

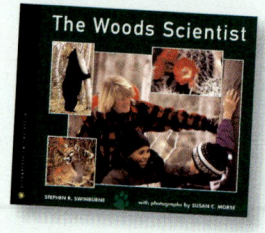

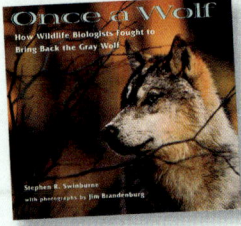

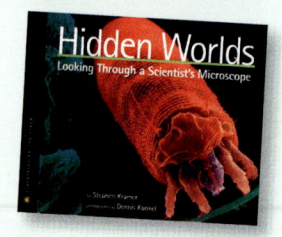

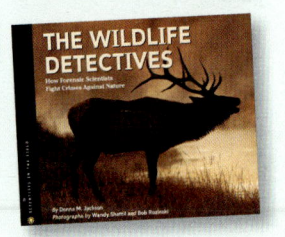

Check out these titles to meet more scientists who are out in the field—and contributing every day to our knowledge of the world around us:

- Chasing Cheetahs
- The Tapir Scientist
- The Snake Scientist
- The Manatee Scientists
- The Polar Bear Scientists
- Stronger Than Steel
- Kakapo Rescue: Saving the World's Strangest Parrot
- Project Seahorse
- The Bat Scientists
- The Elephant Scientist
- The Frog Scientist
- Saving the Ghost of the Mountain: An Expedition Among Snow Leopards in Mongolia
- Whaling Season: A Year in the Life of an Arctic Whale Scientist
- The Mysterious Universe
- Science Warriors: The Battle Against Invasive Species
- Emi and the Rhino Scientist
- The Whale Scientists: Solving the Mystery of Whale Strandings
- Diving to a Deep-Sea Volcano
- Quest for the Tree Kangaroo: An Expedition to the Cloud Forest of New Guinea
- Tracking Trash: Flotsam, Jetsam, and the Science of Ocean Motion
- The Prairie Builders
- The Tarantula Scientist
- The Woods Scientist
- Once a Wolf: How Wildlife Biologists Fought to Bring Back the Gray Wolf
- Hidden Worlds: Looking Through a Scientist's Microscope
- The Wildlife Detectives

Looking for even more adventure? Craving updates on the work of your favorite scientists, as well as in-depth video footage, audio, photography, and more? Then visit the new Scientists in the Field website!

www.sciencemeetsadventure.com